Language, Literacy and Children with Special Needs

SALLY M. ROGOW

Pippin Publishing

Copyright © 1997 by Pippin Publishing Corporation
85 Ellesmere Road
Suite 232
Scarborough, Ontario
M1R 4B9

Edited by Dyanne Rivers
Designed by John Zehethofer
Printed and bound in Canada by Friesens

Canadian Cataloguing in Publication Data

Rogow, Sally M., 1930-
    Language, literacy and children with special needs

(The Pippin teacher's library)
Includes bibliographical references.
ISBN 0-88751-072-8

1. Handicapped children - Education - Language
arts. 2. Handicapped children - Education (Primary).
I. Title. II. Series.

LC4028.R64 1997   371.91   C97-930278-1

ISBN 0-88751-072-8

10   9   8   7   6   5   4   3   2   1

CONTENTS

Acknowledgments

The experiences described in this book are real, but the names of the children, the teachers and other identifying data have been changed. The children shared their stories and the teachers shared their insights and experiences. Without their willingness to do so, this book could not have been written.

I am especially indebted to Tom Cowper, Ruby Dahl, Cathy Humphries, Sharon Henderson and Florence Westbrook for sharing their experiences with integrating children with disabilities in primary classrooms. To my husband, Bob, who listened, encouraged and read through the many versions of this book, my deepest appreciation. To Lee Gunderson and Jon Shapiro, thank you for your support and belief in this book.

A special thank you to my editor, Dyanne Rivers, who steered the book to completion with sensitivity, insight and painstaking effort.

. . . .

INTRODUCTION

"He plummeted into language like an avalanche, as if it were his one escape route from death—which, of course, it was. He had been locked for years in the coffin of his body, unable to utter. When he found words he played rapturously with them, making them riot and lark about, echoing, alliterating and falling over one another."

John Carey
Preface to *Under the Eye of the Clock*

This is how John Carey described Christopher Nolan in his preface to the British edition of Nolan's fictionalized autobiography, *Under the Eye of the Clock: The Life Story of Christopher Nolan*. Nolan is an Irish poet who was born with severe physical disabilities. His movements are uncoordinated and he can neither walk nor talk. No one knew of his gift for language until he was given a computer when he was 11 years old. *Dam-Burst of Dreams* was his first published work and includes the poems he wrote before he was 15.

Nolan's parents never doubted his intelligence. His mother covered the walls of her kitchen with letters of the alphabet, words and phrases. The following is Nolan's own description of how his father's vivid stories and poems stirred his imagination and inspired his love of language:

"(My father's) eye would spot fresh reminders of hidden stored poetry, and true to notational nurturing he'd borrow lines which would unconsciously nurse his family into his luxurious landscape. So it was that his children culled musical notation, intricate thought patterns and a merry love of writing."

Helen Keller, writer, social commentator and leader in establishing services for blind people, was both blind and deaf.

She lost her sight and hearing when she was just one year old. As the small Helen grew into a wild and unruly child, her desperate parents sought help from the Perkins School, a famous school for the blind near Boston, Massachusetts. Michael Anagnos, the school's superintendent, suggested that Anne Sullivan Macy, a young teacher, live at the Keller home in Tennessee and teach Helen. When Sullivan arrived, she found a stubborn and desperately unhappy little girl who stumbled around the house knocking down everything in her way. Patiently and persistently, Sullivan led her pupil out of her confusion and personal turmoil by shaping words on the palms of Helen's hands. In *Teacher: Anne Sullivan Macy*, Keller gave her younger self, the self who did not know language, a name—Phantom:

> "Phantom did not seek a solution for her chaos because she knew not what it was. Nor did she seek death because she had no conception of it. All she touched was a blur without wonder or anticipation, curiosity or conscience. If she stood in a crowd, she got no idea of collective humanity. Nothing was part of anything, and there blazed up in her frequent, fierce anger which I remember not by the emotion but by a tactual memory of the kick or blow she dealt to the object of that anger. In the same way I remember tears rolling down her cheeks but not the grief. There were no words for that emotion or any other, and consequently they did not register."

To the small Helen who could not see or hear the world, the first words she learned were like "beams of sunlight that penetrate the darkness."

Christy Brown, the Irish novelist, could not walk or articulate words clearly. Like Christopher Nolan, he was born with a severe form of cerebral palsy. In his autobiography, *My Left Foot*, Brown described the incredible elation he felt when he discovered he could print with a piece of chalk stuck between his toes:

> "That one letter scrawled on the floor with a broken bit of yellow chalk gripped between my toes, was my road to a new world, my key to mental freedom. It was to provide a source of relaxation to the tense taut thing that

was me which panted for expression behind a twisted mouth."

Many other people with disabilities have also written accounts of how they learned to read and write. In every case, they were supported by persistent teachers and parents who refused to allow disability to interfere with the child's mental and social development.

Literacy is a door to the world, as well as a means of communication and achievement.

Literacy Instruction and Children with Special Needs

As school administrators recognize the right of all children to attend their neighborhood school and feel accepted and valued in their community, they are adopting policies designed to include children with special needs in mainstream classrooms. As classroom teachers accept and encourage these inclusion policies, however, they are finding that responsibility for ensuring that children with special needs are successfully integrated into the school community is falling directly on their shoulders. This leaves teachers to cope with issues that have no simple or easy resolutions. As a result, they have many questions:

— How can I provide for a child with a developmental disability without compromising the integrity of my program?
— How can I involve an inattentive and restless child in storytelling?
— How can I help a blind student participate in projects with her classmates?
— How can I adapt materials for a child who cannot turn the pages of a book?
— What can I expect of a child whose language development is severely delayed?
— Can a child with a learning disability learn to read in a whole language classroom?
— How do I teach composition skills to a child who cannot write?
— How can I help the other children in the class be more understanding of the child with special needs?

These are difficult questions, and the answers depend on the individual child—the type and degree of disability, the child's background experiences, and the positive expectations and opportunities that teachers provide.

For any child, learning to read and write is a process of learning to think about language and understand how printed symbols represent the language we hear. It draws upon a range of abilities and builds upon children's background knowledge, language and experience. And because children become readers and writers with adults who read and write with them, shared reading experiences play an important role in shaping children's knowledge and understanding of words in print. Listening to books read aloud is the cornerstone of literacy.

Teachers know how important it is to enable children to bring what they already know to the task of learning something new. They demonstrate what and how to learn and help children make connections between the language they hear and the language they see.

A child who is listening expertly uses the same senses and techniques as a mature reader. In *Five to Eight*, Dorothy Butler says, "She is able to absorb and process a stream of language, arranging ideas so that the author's message is understood and building, step by step, a mental picture of the whole."

The fundamental principles and practices of literacy instruction apply to *all* children, whether they have special needs or not. All children learn when they have opportunities to:

— Listen to books and stories read aloud.
— Hear the complex language patterns of literature.
— Use their own experiences and their own language as a foundation for building concepts about oral and written language.
— Participate in storytelling activities with other children.
— Discover that ordinary speech can be recorded in printed letters and words.
— Organize and express their thoughts in writing.

As children with special needs become integrated into mainstream classrooms, ensuring that they share in opportunities to do these things presents a special challenge to teachers.

Mrs. G teaches six- and seven-year-olds in an elementary school in a large city. She values the time she spends sharing books with her class; the children gather round her on the carpeted floor and eagerly respond to the reading with comments and questions. Henry, a six-year-old boy whose development is delayed, sits quietly with the other children, but rarely speaks and gives no indication that he comprehends. Mrs. G has no idea whether Henry understands the books she reads to the children.

Charlie literally bounded into Mr. A's class of seven- and eight-year-olds during morning storytime and loudly announced, "I'm here, Mr. A. I forgot my lunch today and had to go back home to get it." Some of the children laugh at Charlie, but others are annoyed by his frequent interruptions. Charlie is restless and inattentive. His writing is illegible and he stumbles over words he managed to read competently just the day before. Mr. A is bewildered and frustrated by Charlie's lack of progress.

A classroom aide wheeled Wendy into Mrs. F's first-grade classroom. The aide helps Wendy eat, go to the bathroom and participate in classroom activities. Mrs. F knows that Wendy enjoys listening to her read aloud in the classroom, but she wonders how this child will become an independent reader. Wendy cannot hold a book, turn pages by herself or paint and draw. Mrs. F has never worked with a child with such severe physical disabilities and she wonders if Wendy can learn to read and write.

Mrs. L is an experienced teacher who has been teaching six- and seven-year-olds in a small rural school district for many years. Most of the children arrive at school by bus. Maud is visually impaired and lives in a small farming community on the outer edge of the school district. She has never been to school before. Mrs. L observes the little girl with the thick eyeglasses and wonders how she will be able to participate in activities with other children. The itinerant teacher for the visually impaired from a neighboring district is coming to consult, but Mrs. L isn't even sure what questions to ask.

This book is for teachers like Mrs. G, Mr. A, Mrs. F and Mrs. L, who are working in primary classrooms with children with disabilities and other special needs. Its purpose is to help teachers find ways to enable these children to learn to read and write together with their peers.

Each chapter focuses on a different aspect of learning to read and write. The first chapter, titled "Everyone Can Learn to Read and Write," discusses emergent literacy and highlights strategies that enable children to find meaning and relevance in print materials and participate in classroom activities. Encouraging active listening and responding to literature are explored in the chapter titled "Story and Storytelling." The aim of this chapter is to show how live storytelling, story retelling, puppet dramas and creative storywriting help children develop their concept of story. The next chapter, "The Sense of Nonsense," addresses language awareness and how playing with nonsense words and phrases can develop children's awareness of rhyme and the sounds that make up words. It discusses the importance of phonological awareness and explores ways of helping children discover that words are composed of sounds and syllables. Learning to organize and express ideas in writing is explored in the chapter titled "Learning to Write." This chapter also discusses how computers can be used to teach writing and the special uses of computers with children who have problems with handwriting.

"Word Knowledge and Reading" discusses vocabulary development as a component of reading with fluency and understanding. It describes strategies for helping children develop an awareness of the structure and meaning of words. By examining how books about children with disabilities can foster acceptance and friendships in the classroom, "Using Children's Books to Promote Understanding" explores how literature can help children develop a sense of identity and self-worth.

Children with severe speech and language problems pose special challenges. The chapter titled "Including Children Who Cannot Speak" describes how augmentative communication techniques and supplementary literacy programs can be used in the classroom. It concludes by describing various inclusion practices and the roles that special education teachers, resource and itinerant teachers, therapists and classroom aides can play in helping teachers ensure that children with special needs are successfully integrated into their classrooms.

The final chapter, "Including Children with Special Needs," discusses the resources that are available to help classroom teachers and outlines some principles that can be used to guide planning and assessment.

The book concludes with a glossary of terms, a bibliography and a section outlining additional readings and resources, including computer software, that can be used with children with special needs.

More than anything, I hope this book demonstrates that when children with special needs are included in primary classrooms, everyone benefits. All the children learn to respect and feel comfortable with their differences; teachers develop their creativity and find new ways of stimulating, enriching and enhancing literacy instruction; and the children with special needs experience acceptance, equality and friendship with their peers.

. . . .

EVERYONE CAN LEARN
TO READ AND WRITE

"Members of the literacy club are people who read and write,
even the beginners, and the fact that one is not very competent
yet is no reason for exclusion or ridicule. A newcomer is the same
kind of person as the most proficient club member, except that
he or she hasn't yet had as much experience."

Frank Smith
Joining the Literacy Club

Lindy, who has a language disability and speaks
in single words or short phrases, seems younger than her six
years. Perhaps because she has difficulty expressing her
thoughts in words, she rarely engages with the other children
in her class, preferring instead to watch from the sidelines. She
spends most of her time painting at the easel or scribbling with
crayons.

Jason has a mild form of cerebral palsy and walks with the
aid of crutches. This six-year-old cannot write or draw. Although he speaks clearly, he rarely initiates conversations
with the other children in his primary class. His teacher, who
taught his brother two years earlier, knows his family and
does not understand Jason's reluctance to participate in activities with other children.

Blind from birth, six-year-old Joy has enrolled in school for
the first time. When her teacher, Mrs. K, visited Joy at home,
she was impressed by this friendly girl's animation and ability
to converse. But she wonders how Joy will be able to participate in literacy activities with the other children. Joy is learning to read and write in Braille with the help of the district's
itinerant teacher for visually impaired children.

How can teachers ensure that children like Lindy, Jason and Joy are able to participate in the full range of literacy activities in primary classrooms?

The initial steps toward literacy are taken long before children enter school. Becoming familiar with books—handling them, looking at the illustrations, and choosing them from the library—teaches children a great deal about print. These early experiences with books develop children's expectations that they will learn to read and write.

Teachers use the knowledge children already possess as a foundation for introducing literacy activities. Children who have been read to at home know that books provide a context for sharing experiences, adventures, images and emotions. From watching their parents read, they know that words tell the story and that they are read from left to right and from the top to the bottom of the page. Furthermore, frequent exposure to the print in the environment shows them the many uses of print. They know about signs, posters, letters, magazines and newspapers and they recognize the logos and names of shops and restaurants. Children with this kind of background come to school armed with the knowledge that printed words have meaning. This background knowledge provides a strong base that teachers can use as a connection to new experiences and new information.

Physical disabilities, visual impairments, language disorders and other developmental problems tend to obscure or distort normal developmental patterns. Children can experience only what they can see, feel and actively explore. Learning takes a different path for children who cannot see or move freely within their environment. Developmental milestones may be delayed, or missed entirely. Familial overprotection and concerns for safety may further limit the social and exploratory experiences of children with special needs.

Some children have learned to depend too much on adults and have had few opportunities to play and interact with other children before coming to school. In *Early Literacy*, Joan Brooks McLane and Gillian Dowley McNamee say, "Play is the arena where connections are made between the immediate personal world and the activities that are important to the larger social world. Play is the context in which many children find ways to make culturally valued activities part of their own personal experience."

Sharing meaning through play, storytelling and other life events is an important building block of literacy. By pretending, children learn to create and share meaning with other children. In their dramatic play, they learn to accommodate one another's interests, weave language into play, and develop their narration skills.

Helping Lindy, Jason and Joy Join the Literacy Club

Teachers who encounter children like Lindy, Jason and Joy for the first time often feel they know too little about children with special needs. They have many questions and concerns. Lindy's teacher wondered how she could motivate her to participate in storytime activities. Jason's teacher was troubled by his lack of initiative and independence. Joy's teacher knew very little about Braille and wondered how she could include a blind child in reading and writing activities with other children.

Teachers depend on the responses of the children in their classes to guide their planning. The steady stream of children's responses keeps them informed about what and how the children are learning. But children with special needs do not always give the kind of feedback teachers are used to. This leads them to wonder how to assess the appropriateness of activities. What kinds of materials do they need to provide? How can they adapt the regular curriculum? Can the instructional needs of children like Lindy, Jason and Joy be met in ways that are consistent with their aims and expectations for other children?

Although the teachers involved with Lindy, Jason and Joy knew that the answers to questions like these vary with individual children and the nature of their disabilities, they felt they needed some kind of map to guide their planning. As they read through the many reports on these children—reports by psychologists, speech-and-language clinicians, and special education experts—they realized that they knew very little about what Lindy, Jason and Joy were really like and what they were able to do. While the professionals who supplied the reports were cooperative and helpful, all three teachers realized that they needed to find out for themselves what each child could do in the context of their particular classroom. And all three were determined that the literacy activities they had planned for the other children would also provide the framework for planning for Lindy, Jason and Joy. Each teacher had three main objectives:

— To involve the child with special needs in listening and responding to stories with other children.
— To use the stories read in class to encourage the child to interact with the teacher and the other children.
— To help the child learn to be independent and self-motivated.

To help achieve these objectives, the teachers, parents, special educators, therapists and classroom aides who were involved with each child met to develop an individualized education plan. This plan defined each child's special needs and specified individual goals. Because Lindy's special needs included speech and language therapy, for example, the speech-and-language clinician worked with her at the school. A classroom aide helped Jason participate in classroom activities every morning. Joy was learning to read and write Braille with the itinerant specialist in the district. The teachers were involved both in writing the plan and making sure that the individualized instruction the children would be receiving was relevant to the activities that took place in their classrooms.

Shared Reading and Writing: Lindy's Story

Ms W, Lindy's teacher, wanted this quiet, withdrawn child to share experiences and ideas with the other children, enjoy listening to stories, and participate in reading activities. To encourage all the children to anticipate and predict story events and to draw their attention to language and the way it creates "pictures in the mind," she frequently read aloud books with strong repetitive language patterns. One day, as she was reading Robert McCloskey's *Make Way for Ducklings*, she noticed that Lindy was paying attention and smiling when she heard a particular passage that evoked strong images of traffic.

Ms W invited the children to describe the pictures they saw in their minds when they heard the words "Honk, honk went the speeding cars." One child remarked that he could hear traffic sounds in the words. They compared the sentence "There was a lot of traffic in the streets," to "Honk, honk went the speeding cars." When Lindy joined the other children in repeating the phrase, "Honk, honk went the speeding cars," Ms W was delighted.

Later, when the children were writing or dictating stories about traffic, Lindy indicated that she too wanted to create a story. Ms W used a modified cloze or sentence-completion technique to help her do this. She started each of the following sentences, then encouraged Lindy to complete it.

I like to watch "the traffic."
I like to hear the "sounds of cars."
I hear the cars go "whish."
I hear the horns go "toot, toot."
I cross the street when the light is "red."

The children also wrote or dictated sentences to describe their paintings and drawings. Although Lindy's artwork consisted only of splashes of color, with no people or objects, Ms W observed that she applied the paint carefully and kept the colors clear, and concluded that the paintings were far from haphazard. She suggested to Lindy that she use her paintings to make a book of colors.

When Lindy said, "I paint colors. I paint red, orange, blue and green," Ms W wrote her comments on the paintings. She also wrote the names of the colors on separate pages, using markers that matched the colors Lindy had used. Then, she placed these pages next to the paintings and encouraged Lindy to point to and read the color words.

Every day for the next few days, Lindy painted another picture in a different color. When she finished, Ms W gathered the paintings into a three-ring binder and placed Lindy's color book in the library corner alongside the books made by the other children.

Ms W also printed Lindy's color words on white cards. After Lindy read them, she carefully placed them in the box that served as her word bank.

When it was her turn to choose a book for class reading, Lindy selected *Goodnight Moon* by Margaret Wise Brown. She sat still for the entire reading and, later, Ms W noticed that she looked at the book again in the library corner. Holding the book in her arms, Lindy said, "The book tell about night. It get dark in night."

When Ms W asked if she would like to make her own book about the night, Lindy nodded and said, "Lindy make goodnight book."

Lindy's mother took photographs of her bed, dresser, toy shelf and teddy bear. Lindy carefully glued the pictures on colored construction paper and dictated a few sentences about each. Here are some of them:

> This is my bed. I sleep in my bed.
> This is my dresser. It has clothes inside.
> I have a lamp on my dresser. It is white. I see my lamp in the dark. Lamp stays on all night.
> This is my teddy bear. He sleeps with me.

Titled *Lindy's Goodnight Book*, Lindy's creation was admired by the other children who wanted to make their own. One child drew pictures of his room on dark paper, another drew a window through which the moon and stars were visible, and still another drew a picture of people sleeping in their beds. Ms W used the variety of goodnight books to talk about how a single idea can be expressed in many different ways. Lindy spoke up in class for the first time when she said, "We make different books, but we all show nighttime."

Ms W encouraged the children in her class to write every day, often about classroom activities. Although Lindy was not able to shape letters, Ms W was determined not to let this prevent her from participating in writing activities.

Although the classroom aide was teaching Lindy to use a computer with an adapted keyboard, a touch-sensitive screen that has a space for every letter of the alphabet and punctuation mark, Ms W also used a variety of other strategies to encourage her to write. Sometimes, she encouraged Lindy to dictate her comments. For example, after washing the paint jars one day, Lindy dictated, "Lindy washed the paint jars. Lindy used soap. Lindy cleaned up." Ms W printed these comments in Lindy's journal and read them aloud to her.

At other times, Ms W encouraged Lindy to write using alphabet stickers, letter stamps and stencils. When the class was planning a trip to the supermarket to buy the ingredients for making Halloween cookies, for example, Lindy looked at the words printed on the chalkboard—"flour," "sugar," "butter" and "eggs." Then, using the letter stamps, she carefully printed "sugar" and "eggs" on her own.

When Ms W suggested that the children choose their own themes to make alphabet books, Lindy decided to make a book about McDonald's. With Ms W's help, she made *My McDonald's ABCs* and pasted a picture of Ronald McDonald on the cover. Her book was typed and placed in the library corner with those of the other children.

Ms W discovered that providing sentence frames was another strategy that worked well because it helped Lindy formulate complete sentences. When she gave Lindy the sentence frame "I like to…," Lindy came up with the following story:

Things I Like to Do
by Lindy

I like to swim.
I like to eat.
I like to shop.
I like to play.

When the children were writing about themselves, Lindy dictated the following story about herself and illustrated it with photographs and pictures cut from magazines and coloring books.

This is me.
I like pictures.
I like ice cream and popcorn.
I like birds and horses.

Lindy dictated a similar story about her mother for her writing journal.

As Lindy's confidence grew and she began to participate in activities with the other children, Ms W was pleased to see her start asking others for help. One day, for example, she overheard Lindy ask another child to help her choose the alphabet stickers to spell "mother," "father" and "baby" for a book about her family.

Ms W was delighted with Lindy's progress and her eagerness to work with other children.

Although she made a point of praising children who helped Lindy, Ms W discouraged them from doing her work for her. By ensuring that all the children had access to the alphabet stickers, stamps, magnetic letters and the supply of pictures, she avoided creating hard feelings by seeming to give Lindy special privileges.

Lindy's classmates also noted her progress. "Lindy's learning to do the same stuff as us," one of the children remarked one day.

Encouraging Independence: Jason's Story

Although Jason was unable to write or draw as a result of his cerebral palsy, his teacher wanted to encourage him to do as many things as possible on his own and join in activities with the other children. Although Mr. H had observed that Jason clearly enjoyed listening to taped books in the library corner, he also noted that he had trouble turning the pages of books and, as a result, rarely read them on his own.

Fortunately, the classroom's library corner also included several books in the Golden Sound Stories series. Printed on thick cardboard, the pages of these books include battery-operated sound strips. When Mr. H gave him *Winnie the Pooh*, Jason was able to press on the sound strips and listen to the sound effects. With some help, he matched the picture symbols on the sound strips to the symbols in the text. And, because the thick cardboard pages were easier for Jason to turn, he was able to look at these books by himself.

To enable Jason to look at other books on his own, the classroom aide duplicated other books and glued the copied pages to cardboard. Keep in mind that this strategy violates the author's and illustrator's copyright. Before photocopying anyone's work, check to see whether your school district has an agreement with a copyright collective. If no agreement exists, teachers can either contact the copyright holder—in the case of picture books, this usually includes both the writer and illustrator—to ask permission to make a copy of the book, or buy another copy of the book to cut up.

When the children were writing or dictating stories, Jason dictated the following story about building trucks to Mr. H and illustrated it with pictures of a bulldozer, a backhoe, a cement mixer and a crane. Mr. H supplied the pictures.

This is a story about building trucks. Backhoes and bulldozers clear the land. Dump trucks take the dirt away.

The bulldozers make big holes. The cranes help the work-men build tall buildings. They need cement mixers too. Building trucks are strong.

One of the children helped Jason glue the pictures of trucks to cardboard pages and the book was placed in the library corner with the books made by the other children.

Jason knew the letters of the alphabet and was learning to use a computer with an adapted keyboard. He dictated his Halloween story to the classroom aide, then read it with Mr. H's help:

There once was a bat. His name was Leo. He went on a walk. He went trick-or-treating. He doesn't have a cos-tume. He got kicked out of the house. He decided to go down their chimney. He flew up to the roof. He climbed down the chimney. He flew right out of the fireplace before the flame could even catch him. The bat got caught by somebody's fish net. He bit his way out. He broke through the window, and flew right back to his cave in the forest.

Mr. H attributed Jason's success to his increased access to materials and activities.

Learning to Work with Letter Symbols: Joy's Story

Because she hadn't attended a pre-school program or Kinder-garten, Joy had few opportunities to play with other children before entering a mainstream primary classroom. Her grand-mother looked after her during the day and often read to her, but Joy had never seen books written in Braille.

The itinerant teacher made Braille labels and signs for class-room use and attached them next to the printed labels on the toy shelf, the art center and the library corner. She also made Braille name tags for the other children and brought a number of twin-vision storybooks to class. These are printed paper-back books with Braille embossed on transparent plastic pages that are interspersed among the paper pages.

Although these books gave Joy the opportunity to share books with other children, it was impossible to obtain Braille copies of all the books kept in the library corner. To overcome this problem, the itinerant teacher began making books for Joy by gluing objects to the pages or placing them in pockets attached to a page. These books were printed in both Braille and regular print so they could be shared with the other children.

Both Mrs. K and the itinerant teacher were delighted when Joy began to participate eagerly in this activity. When they decided to make a book about sticks and stones, Joy glued sticks and little stones to the pages with the help of the itinerant teacher. Here is her story:

Can you feel these little sticks?
Here they are 1, 2, 3, 4.
Now I'll go and collect some more.
Round stones, smooth stones, and rough stones.
Big stones, little stones, skinny stones, chunky stones.
I like to hold stones in my fingers.
Stones are hard and smooth and cool.
But some are rough and sharp.
I like to hear the sounds stones make.

When Mrs. K introduced a project on environmental sounds, the children dictated or wrote stories about familiar sounds and illustrated them with drawings. Joy's itinerant teacher recorded the sounds of doors closing, cars running, wind blowing, and rain falling to "illustrate" the story Joy dictated for the class book:

This is a story about the sounds around. "Patter, patter, pat" is the sound of rain. My grandma does not like to walk in the rain. So we went into the car. "Slam bam" went the car door. "Slosh, slosh" go my feet in wet puddles. "Slam" goes the door when we go outside the house. We heard the rain go "splatter, splatter."

Joy enjoyed dictating her story and added more sentences about sounds:

AAAAAzum goes the vacuum cleaner.
Brrrrrush goes the broom.
Sizzle, grizzle goes the stove.
Bingle goes the doorbell.

As she learned that she, too, could create stories, Joy dictated her own version of the story of the three bears and her teacher recorded it:

Once upon a time there was a girl. Her name was Goldilocks. She went into the woods. She found a house and went inside. There were three chairs.

She sat on the little chair. Oops, the chair broke.
Then she went to the kitchen and tasted the oatmeal. She ate the little bear's oatmeal all up. It tasted so good.
Then she went to sleep on little bear's bed.

The bears came home. Goldilocks jumped up from the bed. She did not want to sleep anymore if there were bears around.

The itinerant teacher transcribed this story into Braille and Joy illustrated it with bits of furry cloth for the bear faces, three toy bowls, three pieces of wood for the tables, and three pieces of blanket cloth for the beds. Her teacher made a print copy so Joy could share her story with the other children.

In Mrs. K's classroom, morning news time was a special period set aside for sharing news. Mrs. K encouraged the children to state their ideas clearly and be receptive to ideas and questions from others. She worried, however, that Joy's inability to establish eye contact might discourage the others from asking her questions. Her worry evaporated one day when she overheard one child telling another, "Just because Joy doesn't look at you when you talk, doesn't mean that she doesn't like to listen to you."

BRAILLE LITERACY

Braille characters are perceived by moving the fingers. Proficient Braille readers use both hands to make left-to-right movements, using the index and middle fingers as the primary reading fingers. The dot configurations of Braille letters and signs—the Braille alphabet is shown on the following page—must be accurately perceived. If dots are missed, the meaning can change.

Literary Braille is a form of shorthand that includes short-form and contracted words. It includes 189 contractions. Letters of the alphabet represent whole words (e.g., b—but, c—can, d—do, e—every, f—from). Common prefixes and suffixes are also contracted.

Joy's itinerant teacher used *The Mangold Developmental Program of Tactile Preception and Braille Letter Recognition*, by Sally Mangold, to help Joy become an efficient two-handed reader.

This teacher worked with her in the classroom and kept Mrs. K well-informed about Joy's progress.

Joy also learned to write with a Braillewriter, an instrument about the size of a typewriter. A Braillewriter has six keys and a space bar that embosses Braille on thick paper. The itinerant teacher gave everyone in the class a card showing the Braille alphabet and Mrs. K used the Braille letters to demonstrate how letter symbols can be represented in different ways.

a	b	c	d	e	f	g	h	i	j

k	l	m	n	o	p	q	r	s	t

u	v	w	x	y	z

Lindy, Jason and Joy—Joining the Literacy Club

Lindy, Jason and Joy are making progress. Although Lindy's progress is slow, she can read simple words and sentences. Jason has begun to read and write on his computer and Joy is reading Braille books on her own. All three children have become members of the literacy club.

. . . .

STORY AND STORYTELLING

"Storytelling is an exchange of gifts. It is a gift of preparation and imagination from the storyteller to the audience. It is also a gift of shared appreciation from the audience to the storyteller. Such telling and listening to stories stimulates an interest in literature, strengthens language development, and primes the imagination."

Marion Ralston
An Exchange of Gifts: A Storyteller's Handbook

Seven-year-old Donny had meningitis when he was just a few weeks old and did not speak until he was three. His teacher was told that he is mildly mentally handicapped. Donny does not organize his thoughts in speech and is restless and inattentive at storytime. Although he is beginning to recognize a few words in print, he is not yet able to read or write.

Annie is also seven. Because her visual impairment prevents her from seeing objects that are more than a few inches away, she cannot use the illustrations in books as clues to interpreting stories. She is also shy and hesitates to join in group activities with the other children.

Victor is seven-and-a-half. He has a form of muscular dystrophy and is unable to walk, write or draw. Although his physical disabilities make it difficult for him to handle books, he is beginning to recognize familiar words and write using a computer. And, while he is always attentive at storytime, he is a passive listener who doesn't participate in classroom discussions or group storytelling activities.

How can their teachers help these children engage in storytelling activities?

Storytelling is a cornerstone of classroom literacy instruction. Talking about, retelling, dramatizing and creating stories are the activities that connect children to literature and shape their awareness of language. In *Cushla and Her Books*, Dorothy Butler described the importance of reading to children. Cushla, Butler's granddaughter, was born with multiple disabilities and needed to be carried and comforted for hours at a time. Her parents read to her from the time she was four months old. Butler wrote:

> "...before Cushla was born, I would have laid claim to a deep faith in books to enrich children's lives. By comparison with my present conviction, this faith was a shallow thing. I know now what print and picture have to offer a child who is cut off from the world for whatever reason. But I know also that there must be another human being to intercede before anything can happen."

Literature and Literacy

Stories demonstrate the power of language to organize our experiences and shape our thoughts. They can be shared only through language. When young children listen to stories, they use their knowledge of language to develop the sense of narrative that forms the core of their thinking processes.

The language of literature evokes images and emotions and invites a range of responses. Repetitive, cumulative and chronological language patterns, as well as rhyming and rhythmic language involve listeners in the unfolding of a story as they learn to anticipate language patterns.

Threads and connections exist between what children already know and what they bring to a story. They care what happens to storybook characters when they seem real and they can bring their own experiences to understanding them.

Developing Story Concepts: Donny's Story

Mrs. B enjoyed telling stories to the seven- and eight-year-olds in her Grade 2 class. She considers live storytelling important because it sweeps children into the story and involves them in the unfolding of the tale. When she told stories, she encouraged the children to participate by using her collection of costumes and props to dramatize the stories they created with her.

Unfortunately, Donny resisted all Mrs. B's efforts to involve him in these activities. He refused to join the story circle, preferring to wander about the room or stay at his desk. And he was no more interested in the books she read aloud than he was in the live stories. Even picture books designed for younger children did not interest him.

Determined not to give up, however, Mrs. B found time one day to sit with him and tell him a story that was "just for Donny." Here's the story—about a mouse who could not sit still:

Mervid was a little mouse who was always hopping or jumping. He just could not sit still. He even jumped up and down when he was eating.

"Mervid," said his mother, "you must sit still when you eat your Jello."

"Not me," said Mervid. "I can't sit still. I won't sit still."

And guess what? Mervid bumped his plate so hard the Jello rolled off the plate.

"Mervid," said his mother, "you must sit still when you eat spaghetti."

"Not me, said Mervid. "I can't sit still. I won't sit still."

And guess what? Mervid bumped his plate. The spaghetti rolled off the plate and splashed on Mervid's shirt.

His mother cleaned him off and said, "Will you sit still and eat some cake?"

"Oh, no" said Mervid. "I can't sit still. I won't sit still."

And guess what? Mervid bumped his plate and the cake rolled off the table.

Mervid was still very hungry, but he could not keep his food on his plate.

What do you think Mervid should do?

Donny watched Mrs. B's face as she told the story. In response to the question, he said eagerly, "Mervid, sit still." Then he grinned up at her and added, "Mervid like to jump and hop. Sometime I hop too, like Mervid."

Delighted by this response, Mrs. B told him another Mervid story the next day. By pausing and asking questions, she encouraged Donny to help her tell the story. Here's an example of the technique she used:

Mrs. B: One day, Mervid went to the pool, but he didn't know how to swim. (She paused and looked at Donny.)
Donny: He splash in the pool.
Mrs. B: He made so many splashes that the mice could not swim. "Go away, Mervid. We want to swim," they said. (She paused.)
Donny: "Okay. I don't splash no more."

The next time Mrs. B sat down with Donny to tell a Mervid story, a few of the other children joined them. In this way, Donny found himself in a storytelling group and Mrs. B expanded the Mervid tales to include other stories about topics and events that were familiar to both Donny and the other children.

Donny enjoyed the television program *Sesame Street* and Mrs. B observed that he was interested in the puppet characters, Big Bird, Oscar, Ernie and Bert. When he brought a Big Bird puppet to school, several of his classmates admired the puppet and talked about Big Bird, Ernie, Bert and Oscar. When Mrs. B suggested to Donny that they create a story about Big Bird, Jimmy asked if he could help tell the story too. Here's how the session went:

Mrs. B: Hello, Big Bird. I see you are eating an ice cream cone.
Donny: Big Bird like ice cream.
Jimmy: Big Bird eats a lot of ice cream.
Mrs. B: Big Bird began to eat his ice cream when Oscar came along. Do you know what Oscar did?
Jimmy: Oscar said, "Big Bird, give me some ice cream."
Donny: "Okay," said Big Bird.
Mrs. B: Oscar took such a big bite that Big Bird had no ice cream left. What do you think he did?
Donny: He go buy more.
Mrs. B: That's right. But when he came out of the store he saw Oscar again.
Jimmy: Big Bird thought Oscar would eat up all his ice cream.
Donny: He run fast.
Mrs. B: He ran down the street holding his ice cream cone. And what do you think happened?
Jimmy: The ice cream fell out of the cone. The ice cream fell in a big plop on the sidewalk.

Donny: Oh no.
Mrs. B: What did Big Bird do?
Donny: He go back to store.
Mrs. B: He went back to the store to buy another ice cream cone, but he had no more money. What could he do?
Jimmy: He asked the store man to lend him money.
Donny: The store man gave him ice cream. He eat it up fast.

Shortly afterwards, Donny brought a battery-operated truck to school and explained that it had been lost for a long time, but his mother had found it. When Mrs. B suggested that he tell a story about his truck, this is what he said:

> My truck go fast. One day I lost it. It went down the street. I run after it. I did not find my truck.
> My mom find my truck in the grass. I glad to have my truck back.

Mrs. B wrote the story in Donny's journal. When she read it back to him, he pointed to and read the words "truck," "fast," "street" and "Mom." Mrs. B then printed these words on cards that Donny stored in his word bank.

As Donny's interest in stories grew, he joined the story circle. He looked and listened with the other children and was especially attentive to stories with a straightforward story line and strong rhythmic language patterns. For example, when Mrs. B read Esphy Slobodkina's *Caps for Sale*, Donny joined the other children in chanting the refrain "Caps for sale." One day, he brought H.A. Rey's *Curious George Goes to the Zoo* to school and asked his teacher to read it aloud for everybody.

Mrs. B noticed that when she gave Donny a story prop to hold in his hands, he sat for longer periods. Holding something in his hands seemed to help him focus his attention. In addition, following a standard routine for storytelling seemed to help him settle in to listen, so she began announcing storytelling time by chanting the refrain, "Listen, listen. My story is about to begin." Furthermore, scheduling storytelling at specific times during the school day also seemed to help Donny anticipate the activity.

When the children retold stories she had read, Mrs. B listened carefully. She found that listening to their retellings helped her assess their understanding of story concepts, recognition of cause and effect, and awareness of relationships between actions and events. After reading *Harry, the Dirty Dog,* by Gene Zion, she asked Donny to tell her about the story. He simply described single events and made no effort to connect them:

> Harry is dirty. He don't like a bath. He don't like soap. It gets in his eyes.

Mrs. B reviewed the sequence of events with him, then asked him to tell her the story again. This time, he connected the events:

> Harry did not take a bath. He got so dirty. No one could see him anymore. Nobody could know Harry. He was so dirty. So he took a bath and got clean. Then everybody got to know him again.

VOCABULARY

One day, after reading the class *Wait Till the Moon Is Full,* by Margaret Wise Brown, Mrs. B was pleased when Donny provided a perfect opportunity to demonstrate how simple words can have different meanings.

"How can the moon get full?" Donny asked. "Moons don't eat."

"That's a different kind of full," one of the children said, laughing at Donny. "When the moon is full that means something different from being full of something we ate."

"We say the moon is full when it is big and round. But Donny is right. We use the same word when we are full after we have eaten a big dinner," Mrs. B quickly explained, offering support to Donny without reprimanding the other child and creating resentment. She asked the children if they could think of other ways to use the word "full."

"A glass can be full of milk or a closet can be full of clothes," offered one of the children.

"Or a bag can be full of candy," Donny said.

Mrs. B no longer had any doubts about Donny's ability to join in storytelling activities.

Annie was a good listener. This visually impaired seven-year-old had had several painful operations to correct her eye problems and visits to her doctor evoked painful memories. Her mother explained to her teacher, Mr. M, that she often calmed Annie's fears by telling her stories.

She recounted one incident that had occurred when Annie was particularly upset. While they were sitting in the doctor's waiting room, Annie was sobbing. Her mother held her and told her a story about a monkey who played funny tricks on the doctor. He hid under the examining table and grabbed the stethoscope to examine the doctor. Annie stopped crying and laughed at the monkey's antics. When it was Annie's turn to enter the examination room, she greeted the doctor by telling him that she wasn't going to play tricks on him.

Mr. M. noticed that Annie listened attentively, but did not share her thoughts with other children. She was timid and did not seem to know how to engage other children in conversation or play. Annie's school experiences had been interrupted by her eye operations and long periods of recuperation. Although she was beginning to read words and simple sentences, she did not draw or participate in classroom discussions.

One day, as Mr. M was telling the story of Little Red Riding Hood, he was dismayed to see Annie put her hands over her ears and start sobbing.

As Mr. M comforted her, Annie explained, "I hate stories that make me feel so scared."

"But it's only a pretend story," said the child sitting next to her. "You know wolves can't really talk."

"It makes me feel too scared. I don't like it," Annie insisted, drying her eyes.

"I don't like to feel scared either, but it's okay to feel scared when it's only pretend," said Annie's neighbor.

Fortunately, none of the other children made fun of Annie for crying and Mr. M watched her relax as she listened to the comments of her classmates. She realized that she was not the only one to feel scared.

Emotion is a powerful force in helping children connect with stories. The stories that speak to their feelings live on in their minds long after the telling. Annie listened intently when Mr. M read *The Secret Garden* by Frances Hodgson Burnett.

Clearly, Annie was deeply affected by Mary, the main character, and during the class discussion, she said, "Mary was so sad. She was all alone. I get sad too when I am all alone. I think people get grumpy when they feel sad."

Annie paid attention to language patterns and tried to repeat them when she retold stories. Here's how she retold Ludwig Bemelmans' *Madeline*.

Once upon a time, there was a little girl named Madeline. She lived in a house in Paris that was covered in vines. Well, Madeline got very sick. She had a terrible stomach ache. Miss Clavell had to run and run because Madeline was crying. Madeline was very scared. Miss Clavell held her tight. Madeline had appendicitis. She did not like the hospital. When Madeline came home again, she was very happy.

PUPPET DRAMAS

Mr. M helped the characters from the stories he read come alive in the children's imaginations by talking about how they lived, the clothing they wore, and the foods they ate. He encouraged the children to use the costumes and props he had collected over the years to dramatize the stories.

When Annie refused to participate in the live dramas, Mr. M encouraged her to work with puppets. Easily handled hand puppets invite children to dramatize stories without compelling them to make themselves the center of attention. Mr. M often used puppets to help dramatize the stories he read and he urged the children to create their own plays. Puppet plays, like other forms of creative drama, encourage children to think about the feelings and motivations of fictional characters.

The hand puppets were made out of socks or paper bags. Faces and costumes were fashioned from colored pieces of felt and strands of wool. Annie made her puppet out of an old sock, gluing bits of wool to it and naming it Lambchop—"just like Shari Lewis on television."

Annie worked with another child to make a puppet drama. At first, they simply described their puppets to each other:

Frank: My puppet is a lion. He's a friendly lion. He won't bite you.

Annie: My puppet is Lambchop. He feels soft and cuddly. He likes to eat lots of candy.

Annie and Frank talked about the brave lion and the friendly lamb.

Frank: I'm a trick lion and I am going to the circus.
Annie: Come on now and go to school. Your teacher will be mad.
Frank: I told you. I am going to the circus. Here I go.
Annie: Are there lions in the circus?
Frank: Of course, and they are very brave.
Annie: Are you brave?
Frank: Don't talk to me. Talk to my puppet.

As Annie gradually came to realize that she was in control of the actions of her puppet, she became more willing to take chances. The lion and the lamb had a number of adventures together.

Mr. M made a point of talking to the children about the books he read and encouraged them to write in their story journals. He believes that ideas about the motivations of characters become more real if children can identify with them. After reading Robert Lawson's *Rabbit Hill,* a story about a group of animals who are fearful of the people who move into an abandoned house on Rabbit Hill, their home, he encouraged the children to talk about the various animal characters. Annie dictated her comments as Mr. M wrote them in her story journal:

Willie was happy. The big old house was empty a long time. The house was lonely. Willie wanted the people to make a garden. He wanted to eat the tulip bulbs. Mole did not like tulip bulbs. He said Willie was selfish. Willie was not selfish. He was happy that people grow food so the animals will not be hungry.

Although Annie was beginning to share her ideas with other children, she still struggled with her fear of being frightened by stories. She asked another child, "Do you really like scary stories?"

"Sure I do, 'cause they're only pretend and they're interesting."

"But how do you know they aren't real?" Annie asked.

"'Cause they're in a book. They're not really happening here in this room."

"That's true. And you can find out how the story ends," Annie added.

Stories were helping this child deal with her fears.

Creative Storytelling: Victor's Story

Ms S guided the children in her class with questions and comments about the stories she read to them and encouraged them to bring their favorite books to school. Victor, who had a variety of physical disabilities, brought *The Little Engine That Could* and told this story:

> The engine was bringing toys to the children. They did not have any toys. The engine was full of toys. It had to go up a big hill. It puffed and puffed. It kept on puffing and came over the hill. The engine brought the toys to the children. Everybody was happy.

Once he'd finished, Victor paused and added, "Sometimes when I try to do something hard, I can't do it. But if I don't think it is hard, then I can do it. Maybe that is what the little engine did."

Victor had no trouble relating his own experiences to the stories he heard in class. When Ms S suggested that the children pick a favorite fairy tale and explain the feelings of the main character, Victor chose Tom Thumb. He said, "If you are very tiny you would have a lot of trouble doing things. You couldn't use a knife or a fork to eat your food. If you are very tiny, you would need tiny clothes, a tiny house and tiny toys. You couldn't play with regular toys. It is too hard to be tiny."

Creative storytelling encourages children to organize their thoughts, think about story elements such as plot, motivation and scene, and express their ideas. Victor revealed his feelings and concerns in the following story, which he dictated to Ms S:

> One day there was a boy. He wanted to go out of his house. The boy went out of his house. He had a long ways to go. It was getting dark. The boy saw a fox. One little touch woke the fox. The fox put the boy into a cave. He made him fall into a deep sleep. He had a magic oven and put him in. The boy did not like the fox. The fox made

him feel angry. His mother and father woke up the next day and they saw that Victor was gone.

"What happened to Victor?" they asked.

They went right out to look for him. They had to hunt in the forest till they found their boy. He had to tell them about the silly old fox. Nobody could understand that fox. The father took the boy home. He was happy to be home again. The doctor had to go and see what happened to him. The boy lived happily every after.

Next, Ms S encouraged Victor to work on a story with another boy. Here is their joint effort, which they titled "How The Lion Got Brave."

This story is about a lion. He was not brave like other lions. He did not like to scare people. He was also afraid of mountains. One day the lion met a tiger. The tiger was brave. He was not afraid of anything. He was not afraid of climbing mountains. The lion wanted to play with him, but he was afraid.

The tiger said, "Follow me. I will show you how to be brave."

The lion followed the tiger. He stayed out in the rain with the tiger, until the thunder did not scare him. The tiger and the lion were friends.

Ms S often used colorful story charts, story ladders and story boards to illustrate scenes from stories and the sequence of events. To make it easier for Victor to see the illustrations, she cut the pictures from old copies of books and mounted them on the storyboards, which were then placed on an easel next to Victor's wheelchair. In this way, Victor could see the illustrations and participate in discussions about them. Victor also learned to operate a tape recorder and listened to books in the library corner.

Ms S's adaptations enabled Victor to become more active in the classroom. He became an eager participant in storytelling activities and enjoyed sharing and working with the other children, who were also interacting with him.

"Victor tells good stories," commented one of the children.

Donny, Annie and Victor—Understanding Stories

The activities that take place around storytelling enhance the pleasures of independent reading. Talking about stories, retelling stories, dramatizing stories and creating their own stories are all activities that encourage children to bring their personal experiences to understanding stories. Donny's, Annie's and Victor's teachers understood this and searched for opportunities to help these children participate in storytelling activities. The chapter titled "Using Children's Books to Promote Understanding" explores the role of children's literature in nurturing feelings of self-esteem, changing attitudes and encouraging friendships in the classroom.

. . . .

THE SENSE OF NONSENSE:

LANGUAGE AWARENESS

"Here comes a pike
Riding a bike
Followed by a cat—all black—
On a scooter, front to back.
Next five mosquitoes come into sight,
Flying along on a yellow kite."

Folk Rhyme

Johnny is a curious, happy seven-year-old with learning problems. His parents began to suspect that something was wrong when he was two and making no effort to speak. In fact, he didn't begin to speak until he was three and continues to have trouble expressing himself.

Although Johnny is beginning to recognize familiar words in print, he has no idea how to decode words he doesn't know. For example, when his teacher asked, "Which word is bigger, bus or jacket?" he laughed and said, "Everyone knows a bus is bigger. Lots of people go on a bus." And when asked to think of a word to rhyme with "pail," he answered "pool."

Eight-year-old Julie can't seem to remember how to spell the words she does know, nor does she have any idea that words can be separated into component sounds. She can write the letters of the alphabet and takes great pains to shape them perfectly, but she pays no attention to letter sequences and relies on her own invented spellings. Julie wrote this letter to her grandmother:

Der Ganma,
You wll cum to my hus. I want to seeyu. I dunt rite good.
But I want yu ta get a letar. I love yu,
Julie

Seven-year-old Tracy, who is blind, prefers to listen to stories rather than try to read them herself. Although she quickly identifies Braille letters and other symbols, she relies on her memory and gives up quickly when faced with unfamiliar words. She does not associate sounds with symbols and has trouble spelling and decoding words.

All three of these children are having trouble developing their phonological awareness—their ability to hear the individual sounds in words, to detect, identify and remember sounds, and to combine sounds and syllables. This awareness is very important because alphabetic systems of writing link sounds with letters, the printed symbols that represent the sounds. In English, for example, the 26 letters of the alphabet represent the many sounds of our language.

While there is evidence that children develop an awareness of the component sounds—phonemes—of a language only after they have learned to read, there is also compelling evidence that some aspects of phonological awareness develop long before children are able to read. For example, the ability to detect rhyme has been observed in very young children. Usha Goswami and Peter Bryant studied rhyme detection in young children and found that the ability to detect rhyme is the connecting link between hearing words and the ability to detect their constituent sounds.

In *Phonological Skills and Learning to Read*, Goswami and Bryant said, "In our view, a child who recognizes that two words rhyme and therefore have a sound in common must possess a degree of phonological awareness, even if it is not certain that this child can say exactly what is the sound that these words share."

Words can be segmented according to their component sounds or phonemes, syllables, or onsets and rimes.

Phonemes are the smallest units of sound and are represented in English by single or combined alphabetic letters. As children learn to appreciate the relationship between sound and symbol, they become aware that words are composed of phonemes and pay attention to letter sequences.

Syllables, which aren't as easily defined as phonemes, are units of speech that are often, but not always, larger than a single segment and smaller than a word.

Onsets are the sounds that begin words and rimes are the sounds in the final syllable. For example, in the word "string," "str" is the onset and "ing" is the rime. Words that share the same onsets are alliterative and those that share the same rime rhyme. Because most of the first words children learn are monosyllabic, primary teachers are not as concerned with syllables as they are with phonemes.

An awareness of onsets and rimes leads to the discovery that rhymes are often composed of the same letter sequences. Goswami and Bryant note that children who can divide words into onsets and rimes begin to categorize words according to common sounds. They can judge whether words have the same onset or rime. This ability to detect rhyme signals a growing phonological awareness and leads to the making of phonological judgments.

Fortunately, phonological awareness can be developed with practice. And nonsense verse can turn practice into fun. The humorous language of nonsense verse exaggerates rhyme and alliteration and focuses children's attention on the sounds and rhythms of language. Rhymes, parodies, topsy turvies, silly sentences, gibberish, onomatopoeic sounds, and jokes and riddles provide rich opportunities to explore language sounds, structures and meanings.

The Sense of Nonsense

Playing with nonsense verse encourages children to direct their attention to phonemes, syllables and rhymes, which in turn encourages them to think about language. As children join in nonsensical chants, rhymes and so on, they learn to pay attention to language sounds. By rejecting normal usage, nonsense verse actually reinforces the understanding of normal usage. In *Two to Five*, Kornei Chukovsky described how nonsense strengthens the sense of what makes sense: "Being an unacknowledged genius of classification, systemization, and coordination of things, the child naturally reveals a heightened interest in those mental games and experiments where these processes are most in use. Hence the popularity of every variety of rhymed topsy turvies among children down through the centuries."

The structure and rhythm of nonsense verse appeal to children of all ages. Nonsense verse shows children how to play with language, and invent new sounds and meanings. By changing word referents, it contributes to the understanding of words as concepts.

Here are some examples:

Tingle, bingle, bangle, wangle.
Waggle, taggle, scaggle, dee.
Look, look, look at me.

Winey, miney, niney, piney.
Did you ever see something very tiny?

Tribbety, bibbety, zibbety, dee,
Can you count one, two, three?

I scream
You scream
We all scream
For ice cream.

Did you ever see a stringbean on a string?
Did you ever see a turnip turn?
Did you ever see a pumpkin pump?

Do you carrot all for me?

My heart beets for you.
With your turnip nose,
And your radish face,
You are a peach.

If we cantaloupe, lettuce marry.

Weed make a great pear.

Developing Phonological Concepts: Johnny's Story

Ms P, Johnny's teacher, often uses Mother Goose rhymes, which are familiar to many children, to demonstrate that rhyming words share the same letter sequences. One of her strategies involves writing the original rhyme on the chalkboard, then changing the final words to create new rhymes. Here's what she did with "Humpty Dumpty," for example:

Humpty Dumpty sat on the wall,
Humpty Dumpty had a great fall.

Humpty Dumpy rode in a car,
Humpty Dumpty didn't go very far.

Humpty Dumpty took a walk,
Humpty Dumpty liked to talk.

The children then worked with a variety of other Mother Goose rhymes to compose their own verses.

Mary had a little guppy,
Mary wanted a little puppy.

Hey diddle diddle,
The cat cooked on a griddle.

To market, to market to buy a big hot dog.
Home again, home again, jiggity jog.

Johnny dictated "Humpty Dumpty sat in a jeep" to his teacher, but couldn't think of a word to rhyme with "jeep." His teacher suggested, "Humpty Dumpty went to sleep."

"That's a good one," said Johnny, laughing. "I have another...Humpty Dumpty had a dream, He dreamed he was eating ice cream."

He also dictated:

Humpty Dumpty had a drink,
He got a drink from the sink.

Ms P wrote Johnny's rhymes in his journal and underlined the letter sequences of the rhyming words. She focused his attention on "ink" and added "blink," "pink," "wink" and "link" to his list. Johnny then composed the following rhyme:

Humpty Dumpty went to the sink,
Water got in his eye and made him blink.

Working with magnetic letters on a steel tray added another sensory dimension to Johnny's activities. Ms P printed the rhyme "Jack and Jill went up the hill" on a card and then spelled "hill" with the magnetic letters. She showed Johnny how "Jill" can be changed to "hill"—and vice versa—by switching the initial letters. Then, she helped Johnny spell words like "fill" and "will."

After this, she used the letters to spell "cat" and Johnny spelled "rat" and "hat." Two other children joined Johnny to make rhyming words with magnetic letters. Together, they made words that rhymed with "bell," "ball," "sheep" and "fun."

Ms P wrote the words on a sheet of paper and underlined the rimes with a red crayon. Johnny copied them into his journal. As he learned to pay more attention to letter sequences, he made fewer errors.

PHONEMIC CONCEPTS

To further develop the children's awareness of the component sounds of words, Ms P wrote nonsense verses like the following on the chalkboard, read them aloud and encouraged the children to chant them with her:

Abba cadabba, madabba, cazee,
I'm so fast, you can't catch me.

Simbo, mimbo, kimbo, kat,
Did you ever wear a funny hat?

Then, she encouraged the children to compose their own nonsense rhymes. Though he needed a little help, Johnny came up with the following:

Bubble, cubble, fubble, nubble,
I can blow a big fat bubble.

Mandee, dandee, sandee, gandy,
I like to eat lots of candy.

When Ms P encouraged the children to make up rhymes about their toys, Johnny dictated:

Toys are fun.
They make me run.

I have some toys
That are for boys.

My balloon goes in the sky.
My balloon is able to fly.

As Johnny's awareness of individual sounds and words slowly took shape, his attempts to decode unfamiliar words became more successful. Ms P knew he was making progress when he asked, "How come 'fly' is spelled different from 'pie'?"

To encourage the children in her class to focus on rhyme, Julie's teacher liked to read the chants from *Crackers and Crumbs* by Sonja Dunn. During one session, she read "Around the Clock Talk," then suggested that they work with her to compose their own chants about time:

Sometime
Good time
Bad time
Fun time
No time
Winter time
Summer time
Spring time.

When she introduced raps, with their fast and steady rhythms, the children composed their own raps on themes like cleaning up, getting dressed, going to school and playing games. Julie worked with another child to compose the following rap about cleaning up your bedroom.

Clean your room
With a broom.
Scrub the floor with a mop.
Take a rest and drink some pop.

The chants were recorded on tape, then written and included in the class rap book. With Mrs. D's help, Julie composed a rap to practice spelling:

H-O-U-S-E
Is the way to spell house.
Change the H to M, for mouse.
T-R-E-E spells tree.
This is a spelling game for me.

Mrs. D also used other forms of nonsense verse, like the following, to help the children focus on language patterns.

This is a story about Mrs. McLorry.
Mrs. McLorry never looked when she cooked.
She thought a roast was a piece of toast.
So she put it in the toaster instead of the roaster.

She sliced a potato she thought was a tomato.
I suppose that you can guess.
Dinner that night was an awful mess.

After encouraging the children to talk about this verse, Mrs. D suggested that they write their own. Julie worked with a partner to compose the following:

This is the story of Timmy McGee.
Timmy McGee climbed up a tree.

This is a story of Tommy McGoo.
Tommy McGoo went to the zoo.

To call the children's attention to onsets and rimes, Mrs. D worked with the class to create a chart like the following, which demonstrates how words can be divided into onsets and rimes.

str	ing
th	ing
br	ing
w	ing
sw	ing

Once she was sure the children understood, she suggested that they think of their own words and make their own lists. Julie worked with the onset "p" and the rimes "en," "in," "unch" and "ack" to write "pen," "pin," "punch" and "pack." Then, she changed the onsets and wrote the rhyming words "men," "sin," "lunch" and "back." Clearly, Julie was beginning to think about the sounds in words.

To focus attention on initial sounds, Mrs. D demonstrated alliterative phrases by writing them on the chalkboard.

Crumbling cookies
Bouncing beds
Goofy geese
Pretty pigs
Puffy pillows

The children really enjoyed composing their own silly alliterative phrases. Julie worked with "baby," "blue," "silly"and "funny" to write:

baby bugs
blue butter
silly soup
funny fish

FUNNY POEMS

The humor in funny poems often comes from combining objects and actions that don't seem to go together. After reading "Psychapoo," a poem from *Alligator Pie* by Dennis Lee, Mrs. D and the children talked about funny poems and rhyming words. After this discussion, Julie wrote the following:

Henry Tomato was red as a beet,
From his head to his feet.

Henry Tomato walked in the water
and swam in the street,
Henry Tomato forgot he had feet.

Henry Tomato wore a hat,
It was made of spaghetti,
What do you think of that?

RHYMING AND SPELLING

Rhyming words in which the rimes are spelled differently demonstrate the importance of looking at as well as listening to words. To illustrate this, Mrs. D wrote phrases like the following on the chalkboard:

A hare on the stair
After the laughter
Enough stuff

Then she combined "bear," "hair" and "square" into the following verse, which she also wrote on the chalkboard:

What is square?
A bear is not square.
A hair is not square.
Only a square is really square.

During this lesson, Julie remarked, "Spelling is tricky. You can't just listen, you have to look at the words too."

Later, Mrs. D talked about homophones, words that sound alike but differ in meaning. She wanted to show the children that words often need to be seen as well as heard. She did not use the term "homophones," but referred to them as "words that sound alike but look different." Writing "pair—pear," "ate—eight" and "blew— blue" on the chalkboard, she illustrated the pairs with the following silly sentences:

Can you eat a pair of pears?
She ate eight apples.
He blew blue balloons.

When she asked the children to write their own sentences, Julie wrote:

I have a pair of socks. I eat a pear.
I ate at eight o'clock.
I blew a bubble. It was not blue.

This work with homophones inspired a discussion of homographs, words that are spelled the same but pronounced differently when they have different meanings. Mrs. D wrote sentences with "tear," "bow," "dove" and "wind" on the chalkboard.

Tear the paper. She has a tear in her eye.
Take a bow. She has a bow in her hair.
A dove is a bird. He dove into the water.
The wind is blowing. Wind up the toy.

At first Julie was confused, but when she copied the sentences in her journal, she remarked, "I guess you can only know which word to say when you see it in a sentence."

To encourage the children to pay attention to syllables, Mrs. D showed them how to invent nonsense words by adding syllables such as "ally," "ably," "ish," "ing" and "inger" to common words like "talk," "walk," "run" and "drop." She then suggested that the children invent their own words. Julie responded enthusiastically, choosing "drop" as her root word and writing "droppally," "droppably," "droppish" and "droppinger." Mrs. D was pleased to see that Julie remembered to double the final consonant and attributed her progress to her increased attention to the sounds and shapes of words.

Sounds and Spelling: Tracy's Story

The children in Tracy's class were using nonsense verse to develop their awareness of the sounds and shapes of words. While the other children wrote their verses, Tracy, who was blind, dictated this verse to her itinerant teacher, Ms S:

Dabba, dabba, dabba doo.
Do you want to tie my shoe?

Tibba, ribba, dibba dee.
I hope you do not laugh at me

Inky, binky, tinky, winky.
When I'm tired my eyes are blinky.

Gilly, billy, silly me.
I wish I could climb a tree.

Melleger, belleger, twelliger, boo.
I know something I can do.

String, bring, sing, ling.
If I cough then I can't sing.

The Braille notation system has special signs for blends and syllables, such as "sh," "ch," "ow" and "ing." Ms S used the following nonsense verse to help teach Tracy these signs:

Lingers, dingers, ringers, mingers
The little Braille letters are tickling my fingers.
Shack, chack, mack dack,
When I read I tickle them back.

Tracy then wrote this verse for her teacher on the Braille-writer and Ms S made print copies so it could be shared with the other children:

Shappy, chappy, thappy, whappy.
I know my signs so now I am happy.

The children played a game called Did You Ever...? in which they took turns finishing the question with a rhyme such as, "Did you ever...see a clown in town?"

Tracy enjoyed this game and offered, "Did you ever know a snake who liked to eat cake?" Later, when she was working with Ms S, she composed more questions of her own:

Did you ever meet an alligator in an elevator?
Did you ever know the hog who sat on a log?
Did you ever sneeze in a breeze?
Did you ever hear a bird say a word?

Tracy wrote her sentences in Braille and asked Ms S to write them in print so other children could read them.

ONOMATOPOEIC WORDS

When Tracy's classroom teacher demonstrated words that imitate real sounds by writing words such as "boom," "buzz," "jingle" and "crash" on the chalkboard, the children talked about words that "make pictures in your head" and thought of other "sound" words to add to the list. When they were composing phrases to illustrate these "sound" words, Tracy joined in with the following suggestions:

Slippery, sloshy, slushy snow
Sizzly, fizzly, twizzly, guzzly, soda pop
Gooey, sticky, wicky, yucky, glue

SILLY WORDS

Tracy's classroom teacher also made up silly words to show how letters are placed in order to make sounds. As the other children made up their own silly words, Tracy dictated hers— along with their imaginary meanings—to Ms S:

Are you gedonded? This means you are mixed up and don't know something.
Don't get petuttered. This means don't get bothered when you can't do something.
Don't be a potterby. This means don't be a pest.
When I hurry, I get bedurry. This means I don't know where I'm going.
Don't gosherwitz your food. This means don't eat too fast.

TONGUE TWISTERS

To focus the children's attention on initial consonant sounds, Tracy's classroom teacher wrote on the chalkboard:

The cute cookie cutters cut cute cookies.
Did the cute cookie cutters cut cute cookies?
If the cute cookie cutters cut cute cookies,
Where are the cute cookies the cute cookie cutters cut?

Tracy had a Braille copy of this tongue twister and recited it along with the other children. Then, she joined the other children to compose her own tongue twisters. Tracy worked with the letters M and S.

Mushy marshmallows melt in my mouth.
Sticky something's stuck in my shoe.

Braille spellings, which often use word fragments to represent whole words, are not the same as print spellings. For example, the word "people" is represented by "p" and "friend" by "fr." As a result, Braille users need to experience spelling words letter by letter to avoid thinking of them only in their abbreviated form. During a spelling bee, Tracy asked if she could use Braille spellings. Her teacher laughed and told her that if she did, the other children wouldn't know what word she was spelling.

JOKES AND RIDDLES

Teachers who use jokes and riddles in their classrooms quickly discover that they are an important indicator of children's awareness of language. Younger children often try to solve a riddle by offering an explanation, while more mature children look for the trick question. For example, a younger child might respond to the riddle, "When is the ocean friendly?" by saying, "The ocean is only friendly in the shallow part." The answer, "When it waves at you," requires them to recognize and appreciate the two meanings of the word "wave."

Between the ages of six and eight, most children become aware that words can be thought about separately from their referents. This developing awareness is reflected in the fact that they start to "get" riddles and jokes, which rely for their humor on the knowledge that words often have multiple meanings and that sounds can be separated from words.

Knock, knock jokes, for example, demonstrate not only that sounds can be separated from words but also that words can be segmented from sentences.

Knock, knock.
Who's there?
Dino.
Dino who?
Dinosaur.

Knock, knock.
Who's there?
Will.
Will who?
Will you play with me?

Riddles are composed of a trick question and an answer. The answer depends on recognizing the trick in the question.

What does the month of February have that no other month has?
The letter F.

What has leaves but no branches?
A book.

The format of riddles manipulates the phonological, syntactic or semantic aspects of language. Phonological riddles are based on word sounds.

What nut makes you sneeze?
Cashew.

Semantic riddles are based on multiple word meanings.

What has a trunk but never goes anywhere?
A tree.

Syntactic riddles depend on syntax and grammatical relationships.

What has four wheels and flies?
A garbage truck.

Tracy enjoyed hearing riddles and making up her own to pose to her classmates.

Where do pigs keep their money?
In piggy banks.

What is the best way to eat spaghetti?
You have to open your mouth.

Her teacher concluded that Tracy's appreciation of riddles was a good indication of her growing awareness of language. Blind children depend a great deal on language to clarify the world.

Johnny, Julie and Tracy—Language Awareness

Nonsense verse, rhymes, poems, jokes and riddles are forms of language play that provide a rich context for developing an awareness of the structure and meaning of language. By showing Johnny, Julie and Tracy how to play with sounds and words, their teachers were able to foster their awareness of language and enable them to engage in language play with other children.

. . . .

LEARNING TO WRITE

"When students see themselves as writers, they find many opportunities for written communication and they use a variety of forms. Writers learn the most and do their best work if the writing is for a real (genuine) audience and is purposeful."

Mayling Chow, Lee Dobson, Marietta Hurst & Joy Nucich
Whole Language: Practical Ideas

Gloria is a shy and lonely child who rarely interacts with the other eight- and nine-year-olds in her Grade 3 class. After her parents were killed in a car accident when Gloria was three, her elderly grandmother took care of her. A year ago, her grandmother—Gloria's only family—became ill and the child was placed in a foster home. Her grandmother died not long afterwards. Mrs. J, her teacher, was told that Gloria is mildly mentally handicapped.

Davy is a handsome eight-year-old with bright blue eyes and a ready smile. He is interested in sports and has many friends outside school. His previous teacher described him as the class clown and noted that he had trouble finishing his work. Davy's handwriting is illegible—many letters are printed backwards or upside down; in fact, even he cannot read what he writes.

A sociable eight-year-old with limited sight, Jenny reads and writes in Braille. Born in India, she was adopted by a North American family when she was two. Her teacher, Mrs. L, is impressed by Jenny's poise and desire to participate in all classroom activities.

Writing involves communicating and sharing information and ideas through the medium of print. In order to do this effectively, however, children must be able to write coherent, organized, legible text.

The Process of Writing

The writing process involves composing, formulating and connecting ideas in well-organized, grammatical sentences. Control over spelling, punctuation and handwriting is an essential element of this process and an inability to master these skills can prevent children from learning to write proficiently.

For children who have trouble printing clearly, a computer can provide the key to participating in the writing process. Adapted keyboards and switches that bypass the keyboard enable even children with physical disabilities to compose and produce text.

Learning to Compose: Gloria's Story

Mrs. L, Gloria's teacher, encourages the children in her class to share their ideas in brainstorming sessions. During these sessions, she tries to remain in the background, knowing that if she makes suggestions, some children are likely to reject their own ideas in favor of hers. Once the brainstorming is over, the children work in small groups to compose, revise and edit. Errors in spelling and grammar are corrected during the revision stage.

Mrs. L was concerned because Gloria rarely contributed during the brainstorming sessions. Nevertheless, as the children were writing stories about themselves one day for a class book called *All about Us*, she was pleased to see Gloria working intently, clutching her pencil tightly and forming her letters carefully. Unfortunately, Gloria's story didn't reflect the intensity of her effort. She wrote:

> My name is Gloria. I am a girl. I am eight years. I like many things.

Children with little confidence in themselves are often at a loss for ideas. Mrs. L was sensitive to this and realized that Gloria needed guidance and structure to help her develop her

54

ideas. When she gently prompted her with questions about her favorite activities, Gloria responded:

> I like to eat hamburgers.
> I like movies like *The Lion King*.
> I watch television.
> I like to go to the beach.
> I like to help Susan (her foster Mom).

As she recorded these comments, Mrs. L suggested that Gloria use them to add details to her story. Here is Gloria's revised story:

> My name is Gloria. I like many things. I like to go to movies. I saw *The Lion King*. That was good movie. I like to go to the beach and play in the sand. I help Susan set the table and wash dishes.

DEVELOPING AN ORGANIZING THEME

On another occasion, Mrs. L noticed Gloria sitting idly at her desk while the other children were writing stories. Tears welled up in Gloria's eyes when her teacher approached.

"I don't know how to make a story," she sobbed.

"You know more than you think," Mrs. L said gently, suggesting that they write a story together. She then used a small hand puppet to help guide Gloria through the steps of constructing their joint story. The puppet had curly blonde hair, a pretty face and a red velvet dress. Gloria named it Polly.

> *Mrs. L*: Let's make up a story about Polly.
> *Gloria*: She's so pretty. I would like her to be my friend.
> *Mrs. L*: What do you think Polly would say if she could talk?
> *Gloria*: She would say that she's my friend.
> *Mrs. L*: Did you know that Polly loves to sing? She has a beautiful voice.
> *Gloria*: Polly has a beautiful voice.
> *Mrs. L*: She could sing on television or be a movie star.
> *Gloria*: She sang lots of songs. She like to be a movie star.
> *Mrs. L*: She went to Hollywood to sing in the movies.
> *Gloria*: Polly said, "Yes, I want to sing in movies."
> *Mrs. L*: She became a movie star.
> *Gloria*: Polly sang beautiful.

Mrs. L: Did Polly like Hollywood?
Gloria: Polly did not like Hollywood. She wanted to be with her friends.
Mrs. L: Did she come home?
Gloria: She come home. She use her beautiful voice to sing and talk.

With encouragement from Mrs. L, who showed her how to use their conversation to guide her writing, Gloria decided to write a story about Polly. She titled it "Polly Goes to Hollywood":

Polly went to Hollywood to be a movie star. Polly has a beautiful voice. She did not want to stay in Hollywood. She was lonely and she missed her friends. Polly came home and used her beautiful voice to laugh and talk and sing.

Pleased with her effort, Gloria went on to write other stories about Polly. To help her, Mrs. L gave her a list of "thought" words, such as "hope," "know," "notice" and "remember," and "feeling" words, such as "angry," "glad," "happy" and "sad." Gloria copied these words into her word book, then wrote this story about feelings:

This is a story about my feelings. I remember my grandma. I sorry she is not with me. I got worried when she was sick. I got scared in the dark. I am happy Susan put a light in my room. You don't have to feel scared about the dark. You can put on a light. I am not scared any more.

I still sad about Granny. I am happy with Susan and Jeff. They take me lots of places. They have a nice car. I help them too.

After a class excursion to the zoo, the children wrote reports about the zoo animals. In the first draft of a story about monkeys, Gloria wrote:

I went to zoo. I saw a monky. The monky was hapy. Monkys lik bananas. Monkys hav moms and dads. Monkys clim trees.

Working with Mrs. L and another child, Gloria corrected her spelling and grammar errors and revised her story to read:

I saw a monkey at the zoo. I like monkeys. Monkeys have mothers and fathers. They eat bananas. I liked to see the monkey climb the tree. It is nice to see a happy monkey.

As she gained confidence in her ability to write stories, Gloria began to contribute to the brainstorming sessions and refer to her word book for help with spelling. Because Mrs. L believes that the desire to write must come from the child or the writing has no power, she encouraged Gloria to express her own thoughts and praised her efforts. Gloria's progress convinced her that this child's learning problems had stemmed more from anxiety than from lack of ability. Mrs. L knew that the longer children experience anxiety about writing, the more reluctant and fearful they become. The structure and guidance she provided helped Gloria overcome her anxiety.

The Computer as Writing Partner: Davy's Story

Davy deliberately avoided writing, probably because he found it terribly difficult to simultaneously think of ideas, form letters and remember spellings. Although his handwriting improved when he used stencils or traced letters, these techniques were so slow and laborious that they interfered with his ability to express his ideas freely. As a result, Mr. J, Davy's teacher, decided that teaching him to write on a computer was the only way to overcome the obstacle created by his inability form legible letters.

Students who use computers in school write more, write better and become more enthusiastic about writing. In *Insult to Intelligence*, Frank Smith said, "Consider some of the advantages that computers offer writers, not just in facilitating the mechanical acts of writing and of editing, but in making information available just when it is needed."

Using a computer to write has many advantages. Computer-assisted writing is easy to edit and revise, and spelling can be corrected with the help of electronic spell-checkers. Furthermore, a variety of special keyboards can help children who are physically or visually impaired.

On the classroom computer, Mr. J showed Davy how to work a computer keyboard and manipulate a word-processing program. Believing that Davy could learn touch-typing once he had made some progress in writing, he began by simply encouraging him to type using the hunt-and-peck method.

After writing simple one-sentence descriptions of illustrations or photographs, Davy composed his first story:

> My story is about a boy who climed a big montin. He tok his lunch and walked a long time. He trid to clim the montin but he slipt. He kept on climin cause he was not scart.

Although Mr. J showed Davy how to use the computer program's spelling checker, Davy still found it difficult to make his own corrections.

When the children were writing reports on a space travel theme, Mr. J supplied Davy with the following sentence starters to help him organize his report:

> I would like to travel in a...
> Space ships can travel very...
> I would like to go to another planet on a...

One day, when Davy enthusiastically described a family visit to a science museum, Mr. J seized the opportunity to encourage him to write another report. To help with his spelling, he gave Davy a list of words related to space travel—"space ships," "clothing," "rockets," "travel," "gravity," "earth" and "radio." Davy wrote:

> Space men travel in space ships. They eat and sleep in space ships. They eat special food and wear special clothes. You can talk to people in space ships on the radio. I would like to go in a space ship.

When the children were writing reports about their pets, Davy wrote about his dog Ticker:

> Ticker is my pet. He is a German shepherd. He is one year old. He is happy when he sees me. Ticker likes to eat hamburger. Sometimes I share a hamburger with Ticker.

Knowing how self-conscious Davy was about his spelling errors, Mr. J helped him revise the text of this story and correct his spelling. As he became more proficient at using the spell-checker, however, Davy gradually began making revisions on his own.

PLANNING AND REVISING

One of Mr. J's goals was to help the children make their stories more interesting. To help achieve this goal, he sometimes used an overhead projector to display a story, then worked with the class to model ways of improving it. This is one the stories he displayed:

> A boy saw a ghost one night. The ghost was scary. The boy was afraid of the ghost. He did not know what to do, so he ran away.

After reading the story with the children, Mr. J guided them through a discussion that focused on techniques for making it more interesting by including details, such as a description of the setting. As the children made their suggestions, he jotted them on the transparency. Here's how the discussion unfolded:

Mr. J: How can we make this story more interesting? What is the first thing we can do?
Rakhi: You have to give the boy a name.
Mr. J: Why does he need a name?
Jenny: So the story is more real.
Mr. J: Okay, we'll call him Charlie. What else do we need to do?
Bobby: Where was Charlie when he saw the ghost?
Mr. J: Good question. Do you think he was standing outside his house? If he was outside, why did he go outside?
Bobby: He went to give his dog some food.
Mr. J: Now we have a main character and a setting. What else do we need?
Min Ming: We need to know why the ghost was scary. What did he do?
Mr. J: Good suggestion, but how can we make the ghost scary?

59

Min Ming: The ghost makes scary sounds, like "Whoo, whoo" in a funny voice.
Mr. J: That sure would scare me. What else?
Sarah: The ghost moves in a funny way. It comes very close to Charlie.
Mr. J: That makes the story much more interesting.

This kind of modeling demonstrates the importance of detail and description in stories. Afterwards, Davy wrote this story about ghosts for the class ghost-story book:

This is a story about a scary ghost. He had no body. He looked like a sheet. He made scary sounds.

He did not want to be scary. He just wanted to be like the other ghosts. Nobody wanted the ghost to come to their house.

The ghost went to a boy's house. The boy was brave. He was not scared. He gave a cookie to the ghost. But ghosts cannot eat. They do not have real mouths.

Mr. J's demonstrations of writing strategies helped Davy formulate ideas. And Davy's growing proficiency on the computer overcame his difficulties with printing, enabling him to participate in writing activities with the other children.

Learning to Share Ideas: Jenny's Story

Jenny used a Braillewriter to complete her writing activities. Ms W, her itinerant teacher, supplied print copies of her written work for her classroom teacher and her classmates.

When the children in Jenny's class put together a class book about themselves, Jenny's contribution was titled "About Being Blind and Eight Years Old":

My name is Jenny. I am eight and my birthday is July 10. I am blind and my hair is black. My favorite sport is basketball. My favorite hobby is writing.

I like spending time with my family. Sometimes I am shy and sometimes I am not. What I like about myself is that I can read Braille.

Sometimes I wish I could see more things. I don't like it when people tell me I can't do things because I can't see. Some little kids don't think what they are doing when they tease me. I don't like it when some of the kids in my class don't want to play with me at recess.

The things that are good are that I can do a lot of stuff that seeing kids can do. I don't see bad movies. I like to do stuff with other kids.

When her class created a book about the seasons, Jenny wrote about autumn:

The color of leaves are red.
Leaves are always soft and some are hard.
Grass feels very smooth.
Trees feel very sticky, but some are not.
Ice sometimes hurts your hands or your feet when you touch it.
Flowers feel very nice and the little ones start to grow.
Rain feels very wet and hard on my face.

USING RESEARCH AND REFERENCE MATERIALS

While Jenny was able to use the Braillewriter to participate in creative writing activities, a shortage of reference materials printed in Braille posed a problem when the time came to do research. For example, when the class went to the library to find reference materials for a project on whales, no Braille materials were available.

This problem was overcome when Ms W found a book about whales on audio tape and showed Jenny how to use the audio tape of the *World Book Encyclopedia*. Jenny then dictated her report to a classmate, and it was placed in the class book along with the reports of the other children:

Whales are very large water mammals. They live in groups called pods. There are different kinds of whales. Some are called killer whales. Dolphins are a quite a bit smaller than whales. It is interesting to hear the sounds whales make. They make different sounds for different reasons. Whales take good care of their babies.

In addition to using the Braillewriter, Jenny was introduced to a Braille Lite 18. This small computer, with the same kind of keyboard as a Braillewriter, provides both tactile and speech feedback. Working with the Braille Lite enabled Jenny to engage in writing activities with the other children. Fortunately, the classroom had a Braille embosser so that she was able to print her stories in both Braille and standard print.

Computer learning should be enjoyable as well as meaningful. In *Parents, Kids and Computers: An Activity Guide for Family Fun*, Robin Raskin and Carol Ellison list several criteria to be considered when selecting computer software for children. Because effective programs provide children with the tools they need to express their own ideas, the best programs are interactive and foster exploration and creative problem-solving. This is often accomplished by presenting open-ended activities that encourage children to make choices. Some interactive programs even enable children to work in groups so that they can share ideas and solve problems cooperatively. Programs that teach skills in isolation should be avoided.

For those who have trouble drawing their own pictures, graphics software makes it possible to include pictures and illustrations in the body of texts. Using computers with children who have severe disabilities is discussed in the chapter titled, "Including Children Who Cannot Speak."

Gloria, Davy and Jenny—Learning to Write

Rather than focusing on their problems, the teachers working with Gloria, Davy and Jenny explored ways of overcoming their difficulties. Gloria's teacher showed this youngster that she was capable of formulating and organizing her thoughts. By building on Davy's interests, his teacher emphasized the expression of ideas in writing rather than the physical act of writing by hand. And Jenny's classroom teacher worked with the itinerant teacher to enable her to join in writing activities with other children. The more Gloria, Davy and Jenny wrote, the more confident they became.

. . . .

WORD KNOWLEDGE

AND READING

"Our findings suggest the need for a serious look at how to accelerate the rate of vocabulary acquisition, particularly of the less common, literary, abstract words needed for reading, writing, and understanding in grade 4 and beyond. Two questions need to be considered: When should we start teaching vocabulary? And what method and materials would be most effective?"

Jeanne Chall, Vicki Jacobs & Luke Baldwin
The Reading Crisis

One day, eight-year-old Danny confessed to Mr. A, his classroom teacher: "If I could read like other kids, then I wouldn't feel so dumb." Until he was referred for testing when he was seven, Danny's learning disability had gone undetected. The psychologist who conducted the assessment particularly noted his poor scores on tests of verbal abilities. A year later, Danny is receiving specialized instruction from the school's resource teacher. Mr. A is also eager to help him improve his reading skills.

Gentle and soft-spoken, eight-year-old Terry emigrated from Scotland with her family and now lives in a rural area where, like most of the other children, she takes a bus to school. Although she can read familiar words and phrases, she stumbles badly when she reads new material. Her previous teachers suspected that she was mildly mentally handicapped.

Jeremy is a serious little boy with impaired vision. He had surgery to correct a heart defect when he was six years old and could not attend school regularly. Now eight, he is in Grade 3 and having problems spelling and decoding new words. Although he speaks clearly and enjoys listening to stories, he reads slowly and finds reading tiring.

Because the ability to read proficiently depends on a knowledge of words, vocabulary development becomes increasingly important as the language in texts of all kinds becomes more complex. As they encounter more complex language, children who are already having trouble reading are at risk of falling farther and farther behind their classmates. As a result, helping then develop strategies for analyzing words and expanding their vocabularies is essential.

In his contribution to *The Nature of Vocabulary Acquisition*, Michael Graves lists four word-learning tasks:

— Learning to read words used in everyday speech.
— Learning new words for familiar concepts.
— Learning new words for new ideas and new concepts.
— Learning that words can have multiple meanings, and that word meanings often vary with context.

Graves noted that successful readers are able to read nearly all the words in their oral vocabularies by the time they are about eight years old. Children who have problems reading, however, may be able to recognize and use many everyday, familiar words in conversation, but struggle to recognize them when they are reading. Danny had difficulty decoding familiar words; Terry was confused by words she did not recognize; and Jeremy did not have enough experience seeing and using words in print.

Using Word Games to Learn about Words: Danny's Story

Mr. A, Danny's teacher, frequently uses word games to teach word-analysis strategies. Simple crossword puzzles, anagrams, and word-matching, word-changing and word-classification games demonstrate how to take words apart, rearrange them and put them back together. Playing with words this way also encourages children to think about spellings and meanings.

Because Danny avoided playing word games, Mr. A suspected that he didn't know how to play. Because he understood that Danny needed to experience success before he would willingly join the other children, he started by showing him how to play some simple games.

The first involved matching the following familiar words from two lists of simple words:

Toy	Ship
Fire	Boat
Radio	Station
Space	Truck

Danny was able to match "space ship," "fire truck," "fire boat" and "radio station." Mr. A then worked with him to find other combinations and, together, they came up with "space station," "fire station," "toy truck," "toy ship" and "toy radio."

Word-classification games involve sorting words by category. When Mr. A suggested that the children select a category and use the words in it to create a theme, Danny chose food and developed a restaurant menu as his theme:

Danny's Take-Out

French fries
Chili dog
Vegetable soup
Hamburger
Hot chocolate
Spaghetti
Chocolate chip cookies
Pizza

Mr. A also gave Danny word cards associated with baseball, football and hockey. Together, they read the words and sorted them into the three categories.

Baseball: bat, base, catcher, pitcher
Football: quarterback, halfback, fullback
Hockey: skate, puck, stick, ice rink

Another classification game involved sorting words into descriptive categories. Danny dictated his words to Mr. A, who wrote them in his word book.

Cold words: icy, freeze, freezing, frozen, chilly, cold, ice cream, snow, ice, shiver, refrigerator
Windy words: blowing, blustery, howling, cold, sailing
Hot words: sun, heat, warm, roast, steam

Sweet words: sugar, honey, cake, chocolate candy, lolli-pops, marshmallows

When they reached the final category—silly words—Danny made up the words "blobble," "tobble," "tooper," "gooper," "zinger" and "blinger."

Mr. A also encouraged Danny to use the sports words he knew to create word chains like the following:

Baseball...hit...batter...base...first base...second base...third base...home run
Football...touchdown...halfback...quarterback...kick ...score
Hockey...rink...ice...puck...face off

To show Danny how to create anagrams, Mr. A presented him first with pictures. Under each, he printed a short, simple word. For example, from "arm," Danny created "ram" and from "pots," he created "spot." As he caught on, Mr. A dispensed with the pictures.

To vary this activity, Mr. A gave Danny words like the following and a definition. Then, he asked him use the letters of the given word to write a new word to match the definition. The words Danny wrote successfully are shown in the right column:

tow	a number	two
end	a lion's home	den
pea	a big animal	ape
cork	a stone	rock

Another game Mr. A encouraged Danny to play involved changing a word one letter at a time to create new words. Starting with simple words that involved only one step (e.g., changing "tall" to "ball" or "tale"), Mr. A gradually increased the number of steps (e.g., changing "base" to "bale" and then to "ball").

Add-a-letter is a writing game that is played with a partner. Each player is given a set of written directions. Danny played with Mr. A:

Start with the letter "t."
Add a letter to make "at."
Make something to wear on your head. (Danny drew a hat and wrote "hat.")

Ask a question. (Danny wrote, "What is my name?")

To help Danny recognize words within other words, Mr. A gave him a list of words with the interior words written in capital letters—"kNOt," "mANY," "bANk," "lAND," "pONd" and "kNOw." Then he helped Danny recognize and underline the interior words. When he gave him a second list, with no capital letters to help this time, Danny was able to find and write the words inside "shears," "ships," "farm" and "kneel."

Another game involved making new words by substituting initial consonants. Starting with a list of words supplied by Mr. A, Danny changed words such as "task" to "mask," "ball" to "tall," "sink" to "rink" and "mare" to "care."

As Danny's confidence grew, Mr. A began to increase the difficulty of the games and encouraged him to work with his classmates. For example, Danny worked with another child to fill in the missing vowels in lists of words prepared by Mr. A. At first, the lists involved simple challenges, such as "r-ce." Then, they became more difficult, including challenges such as "diff-cult" and "mel-dy."

Danny also worked with another child to play a game that involved combining two words to create new words. Together, the two children combined "number," "coat," "take," "smart," "doors," "last," "rage" and "shoes" with "over" and "out."

By the time Mr. A introduced the secret code game, Danny was becoming less reluctant to play word games with the other children. Mr. A began be showing the children the code, which involved reversing the spelling of the words in sentences he printed on the chalkboard:

Esaelp emoc ot ym esuoh.
Tae ruoy hcnul.

Once he had worked with the class to decipher these sentences, he suggested that the children use the code to write their own secret words, then give them to a partner to decipher. Danny participated enthusiastically. He wrote "candy," "book," "pencil," "paper" and "boy," then carefully printed them in reverse. His partner read these words, then gave Danny his list, which included "sub," "niart," "rac" and "nuf." Once Danny had successfully decoded the words, Mr. A was delighted to hear him say, "When I know how to do something, then I can do it."

Danny played this rhyming game with his class. The clues to rhyming words were given in sentences like the following:

A word that rhymes with "cat."
You wear it on your head and call it a....

A word that rhymes with "keep"
Is a woolly animal called a....

Danny also worked with simple crossword puzzles and discovered that he knew more about spelling than he thought.

Finally, Mr. A used J. Agee's *Go Hang a Salami! I'm a Lasagna Hog and Other Palindromes* to introduce palindromes, words and phrases that read the same from left to right and right to left. When he suggested that the children create their own palindromes, Danny worked with another child to produce "Funny ynnuff," "Anana B. Banana" and "Pull up."

WORD MEANINGS

To encourage the children to think about word meanings, Mr. A often drew their attention to figurative language and idioms. For example, one day he wrote the following list on the chalkboard under the heading Funny Sayings:

Brain waves
Bonehead
Headache
Eye wash
Fellowship
Tune out
Level-headed
Wound up

The children then chose one of the sayings and illustrated it with a sentence and a drawing. Danny chose "bonehead" and drew a picture of a boy with a bone in his head. He wrote, "A bonehead is dumb. He has a bone in his head. He has no brain."

Mr. A also encouraged the children to recognize that common words can have more than one meaning. One day, for example, he wrote a series of sentences on the chalkboard to illustrate the various meanings of "head":

She's got a good head on her shoulders.
The principal is the head of the school.
The train got up a head of steam.
He wants to head the team.
Head into the wind.

He then asked the children to choose a word from a list he presented and write sentences to show its various meanings. Danny worked with "run":

Run for your life. This means run away from something bad.
Home run. The hitter hit the ball and ran to home base.
The train runs on time. The train is not late.
Run, don't walk. This means go fast.

Mr. A's encouragement and praise helped Danny discover his own abilities. He told his teacher, "I guess I'm not as dumb as I thought."

Vocabulary Development: Terry's Story

Mrs. N watched Terry clench the book in her hands as if she thought she could squeeze the meaning from the words and knew the intensity of this shy eight-year-old's anxiety. Terry's family had immigrated from Scotland and she was used to different oral language patterns. Her teacher wondered if this was the reason she had so many problems recognizing words in print.

Mrs. N tried to help Terry feel comfortable in class and encouraged her to talk about her interests. Terry confided that her mother told her fairy stories. "My best story is the tale of the good housewife," she explained. When Mrs. N said she wasn't familiar with this story, Terry eagerly launched into a telling of the tale:

The housewife is a woman. She lived in Scotland. She worked hard. She was tired. She ask the fairy people to help her. The fairy people were tiny. They are called Little People. They came to do the work. The woman she cook for them. She cooked and cooked. That made her tired. She want Little People to go away. She want to be rid of them. They don't go away. A wise man tell her mess your house. Then, the little people come back. She don't let them in. And so they go away and never come back.

Terry's well-organized retelling impressed Mrs. N, who began to suspect that this girl's problems with reading were related to her limited vocabulary and not to a lack of ability. She searched out a book of Scottish fairy tales and read several of them to the class, then guided the children in a discussion of the various terms used to describe the characters. She wrote "fairy," "little people," "faery" and "leprechaun" on the chalkboard. They also talked about the names used for evil creatures, such as "witches," "monsters," "ogres," "hags" and "sorcerers." The children wrote the words in their journals and sorted them into categories.

When the children suggested other categories, such as "magic," "kings" and "palace," Terry copied the words into her journal and listed:

Magic: spell, enchant
Palace: castle, palace, mansion.

She was smiling when she read the words to Mrs. N.

WORD MEANINGS

After illustrating how different words can express the same meaning, Mrs. N divided the class into small groups and suggested that the children work together to find synonyms for various words. Terry's group worked with "happy" and "sad." Although Terry contributed only "not sad" during the group discussion, she listened to the other children and then wrote two lists:

Happy: joyous, glad, ecstatic, merry
Sad: miserable, unhappy, blue, down in the dumps, forlorn

When Mrs. N. talked about antonyms, Terry remarked, "All my words for 'happy' are opposites of my words for 'sad.'"

To encourage the children to think about word meanings, Mrs. N read from *The Play of Words* by Richard Lederer to demonstrate how idioms make language more lively. She then wrote several sentences containing idioms on the chalkboard:

Do you have something up your sleeve?

He's mad. I guess he's hot under the collar.
She's tied to her mother's apron strings.

Several children observed that idioms put pictures in your head. When Mrs. N suggested that children work in pairs to illustrate two idioms with descriptive sentences, Terry and another child worked with "Blow your own horn" and "Pipe down." Terry wrote,

Blow your own horn. A boy bragged about hisself a lot of the time. He blows his own horn.
Pipe Down. The kids was making lots of noise. The teacher told them to pipe down.

NEW WORDS

Terry's teacher sometimes introduced new words by talking about how words can be defined and compared with familiar words. One day, she presented a list of words and asked the children to choose one, compare it with a word they knew, look it up in the dictionary, and use it in a sentence. Terry worked with "country":

Definition: A country can be another land or nation. A country is also a place that is not the city.
Comparison: The country is not like the city. It is more quiet.
Sentence: I live in a country called Canada. I live on a farm in the country.

One day, Mrs. N read Patricia Hubbell's *Word Woman* to the class. Intrigued by this story about a woman who carried words with her in a jar and threaded them to the stars whenever she wanted to travel, Terry wrote a poem about words:

Words are not things you wear.
You don't take them from a jar.
But you say them every day.
You have to know them in your head.
You can think about them in bed.

New Words and New Ideas: Jeremy's Story

Mr. E encouraged the children in his class to keep reading journals and used these to help guide his assessment of their progress. "Keeping a journal is like having a conference with yourself," he explained. At first, Jeremy, whose vision was impaired, dictated his journal entries to a classmate or the classroom aide. He was also learning to operate a laptop computer with a screen adapted for large print so that he could write his own journal entries.

When Mr. E read aloud Robert Lawson's *Ben And Me*, the story of a mouse who helped Benjamin Franklin discover electricity, Jeremy enjoyed the story and wrote in his journal:

> Ben Franklin liked to think he discovered electricity. It really was a little mouse who discovered it. The mouse crawled up Franklin's kite and got an electric shock. That is how Franklin knew about electricity. The mouse did the job. But Franklin wanted people to think he made the discovery. He tried to keep the mouse quiet. But you can't hide the truth.

Although Jeremy misspelled many words, his writing was clear evidence of his ability to organize and express his thoughts. As he observed Jeremy working, Mr. E understood that it was Jeremy's impaired vision, not his intellect, that was interfering with his progress. He resolved to obtain more large-print materials and invited Jeremy to participate in choosing those that would be most helpful.

NEW WORDS FOR NEW CONCEPTS

When he introduces science and social studies activities, Mr. E often teaches new words and concepts before the children encounter them in their reading. When the class was working on a communications theme, for example, Jeremy learned "commentator," "newspaper," "journalism," "reporters," "report," "broadcast" and "media" from the word list Mr. E presented in large type. Jeremy then used these words to write a report on sports reporters:

> A sports reporter writes about baseball, football, hockey and other sports. Sometimes he broadcasts a report on the television or radio. And sometimes he writes for a news-

paper. Sports reporters get to go to all the games. I think they go for free. I would like to be a sports reporter. Then I could go to the games.

I do not have a favorite sport.

During a unit on prehistoric mammals, Jeremy worked with a small group of children interested in dinosaurs. They looked up paleontology in the dictionary and wrote about paleontologists in their journals. Jeremy found the word in his large-print dictionary and wrote his own explanation:

Paleontologists discover dinosaur bones. They dig in the earth with special instruments to find dinosaur bones. It can take them a long time to find enough bones to make a whole skeleton. Paleontologists help us know about dinosaurs.

With the children, Mr. E demonstrated the meaning of the suffix "ology" by examining words such as "paleontology," "biology" and "meteorology." Then he invited everyone to find two "ology" words and write about them. Jeremy looked up the "biology" and "meteorology" and wrote on his computer:

Biology is the study of living things and biologists study them. They study about things that grow and live like animals, birds and fish.

People who know meteorology study the weather. They tell us if it is going to rain or be a sunny day. Sometimes they don't know.

FIGURATIVE LANGUAGE

To introduce a discussion of figurative language, Mr. E read aloud *Mad As a Wet Hen and Other Funny Idioms* by Marvin Terban. After the discussion, each child chose three idioms to explain in writing. Jeremy wrote:

The early bird catches the worm. That means that if you are first in line, you can get what you need.
The boy went on a wild goose chase. That means he couldn't find what he wanted.
It's for the birds. You say that when you don't like something or think it is silly.

Jeremy also wrote about being happy as a clam:

How do you know the clam is happy? He lives in the water. He has a shell to keep him warm. If a clam is warm, then he is happy. When I am warm, I am happy as a clam.

As Mr. E watched a keen sense of enjoyment replace Jeremy's frustration and despair, his belief in the power of motivation to overcome obstacles was confirmed. Because reading long texts continued to be a problem for Jeremy, Mr. E shortened some of the classroom assignments to avoid the inevitable fatigue associated with prolonged reading and also tried to obtain audio tapes of the novels and mystery stories the other children were reading.

Danny, Terry and Jeremy—Vocabulary Development

By joining in all sorts of wordplay with their classmates, these three children increased their repertoire of tools for dealing with unfamiliar vocabulary. Word and spelling games gave Danny the tools he needed to spell and construct words. Terry increased her vocabulary, as well as her interest in word meaning. And Jeremy's abilities were given expression in the classroom. As they learned to decode words and use them in their own writing, their confidence in their ability to read and write grew and they began to participate more actively with the other children, an important social effect that will be examined in greater detail in the next chapter.

USING CHILDREN'S BOOKS

TO PROMOTE UNDERSTANDING

"(My friends) were there, close to me, with me. They asked me questions, and I asked them in turn. They helped me live as if I had eyes, to learn to climb trees, to row a boat, and sometimes to steal apples. And to their surprise and often my own, I taught them to see better."

Jacques Lusseyran
The Blind in Society

Born with a severe physical disability, eight-year-old Lori is self-conscious about her appearance. Her spine is malformed and she is much smaller than the other children in her class. She feels ignored by the other children and wrote in her journal:

It makes me sad to realize that no one else has a problem like I have. My teacher wants to help me. But I hate it when she tells the other children to be careful around me. This makes it hard for me to make friends. It makes me angry.

Stanley has a rare allergy to light and must wear eye glasses that look like goggles. He wants desperately to be accepted by the other children and gets upset when they refer to him as "the blind boy." Stanley protested to his teacher, "Don't those kids know I can see a little bit? I can do lots of things that they do. I wish I could see like other kids."

When Harvey was seven, he was badly injured in a car accident. Once an active, popular youngster who loved playing sports, he is now coping with severe physical disabilities and requires assistance with eating and toileting. He told his teacher, "My friends used to come to my house a lot, but now they don't want to spend time with me. I probably make them feel bad. They feel sorry and they don't know what to say to me."

Children who look different or act differently are often lonely and confused. In fact, the emotional effects of a disability are often more difficult to deal with than the disability itself. Because their sense of identity often reflects the way they are treated by their peers, children are quick to sense social distancing and rejection. As a result, achieving a sense of belonging is often painfully difficult for those who are different.

This chapter examines how children's literature can be used to help improve the self-esteem of children with special needs, change the attitudes of other children toward them, and promote acceptance, cooperation and friendships in primary classrooms. When they read and hear stories that relate to their own experiences, children with special needs become more aware of themselves and more able to cope.

In *Children's Friendships*, Zick Rubin noted that it is only in the social context of their peer group that children develop a sense of belonging. Like other children, children with special needs want to feel that they belong, but making friends can be difficult and they are often very sensitive about what others think of them. Some feel that the only way to win respect is to be perfect and never make a mistake. So desperate are they for acceptance that they repress their own feelings out of fear of rejection. Others deny their disabilities, pretending they don't exist.

The responses of classmates to children with special needs are influenced by many factors, including appearance, the degree of disability, and behavior. Too often, a disability label tends to identify a child as "sick" in the eyes of his or her classmates, especially when the non-disabled children feel they can't talk openly about it. Fortunately, literature provides a non-threatening way of enabling children, whether they have special needs or not, to openly express their feelings, fears, confusions, attitudes and expectations.

Deeply personal meanings come from the connections children make between their own feelings and those of storybook characters. Even before children have words for their emotions, they can identify with the emotions of fictional characters. The ferocious lions and tigers, shy and fearful rabbits, brave bears and silly geese in children's literature give form and substance to unexpressed emotions. Deeply personal meanings come from the connections children make between their own feelings and those of storybook characters. At the same time, realistic fiction mirrors children's experiences and demonstrates how problems can be solved and difficulties overcome.

Authors of books for young children, such as Maurice Sendak, address the intensity of emotions in ways young children understand. Sendak's characters, for example, are often locked into rigid forms of behavior and need outside help to overcome this. *Where the Wild Things Are* is a wonderful book for opening discussion with children about feelings.

Fairy tales and folktales are also terrific vehicles for bringing children in touch with their feelings. In *The Uses of Enchantment*, Bruno Bettelheim explained, "The fairy tale from its mundane and simple beginning, launches into fantastic events. But however big the detours—unlike the child's untutored mind, or a dream—the process of the story does not get lost. Having taken the child on a trip into a wondrous world, at its end the tale returns the child to reality, in a most reassuring manner."

A Sense of Identity: Lori's Story

Lori had good reason to feel rejected by the other children. Shunned by most of her classmates, she was really hurt when she overheard one child whispering, "Lori looks like she should be in Kindergarten," and another called her "the humpback."

Lori's shyness and fear of rejection isolated her from the other children and her frequent absences from school for medical reasons made developing social relationships even more difficult. Although her teacher, Mrs. S, knew she couldn't force Lori or the other children into friendships, she did try to include Lori in all group activities. As she got to know Lori, she realized that this lonely child was caught in a vicious circle. Her expectation of rejection kept her from trying to initiate relationships with other children, who, in turn, avoided her because of what they interpreted as stand-offishness.

Lori was an avid reader of fairy tales and Mrs. S decided this interest might be a way of building her self-awareness and self-esteem to the point where she might overcome her shyness and fear of rejection. Lori told her, "Fairy stories are my favorite stories. They take me to magic places. In fairy stories, people's wishes come true and that makes me feel happy."

Mrs. S started by encouraging Lori to write about her favorite stories in her journal:

I like *The Little Mermaid*. The story tells about a mermaid. She wanted to be human and marry the prince. Her legs gave her lots of pain. But she did not care about that. She was brave and good. My legs hurt me too sometimes. I know how that can hurt. In the story she dies so she can be with her sisters. She did not really die. She changed her form again.

I don't mind when stories have sad endings. *The Steadfast Tin Soldier* has a sad ending, but you would not know how brave the soldier was if the story had a happy ending.

After her teacher told the class the folktale, *The Old Woman Who Lived in a Vinegar Jar*, Lori wrote:

That woman is never happy. The fairy tried to make her happy. She gave her the big house she wanted. She gave her a palace. The lady was still grumpy. So the fairy put her back in the vinegar jar. The story tells about being happy with the things you have, but sometimes you can't.

One day, Mrs. S read aloud Becky Reyher's *My Mother Is the Most Beautiful Woman in the World*, the story of a Russian girl who sets out in search of her mother, from whom she has been separated. As the girl wanders from village to village, people ask what her mother looks like and she responds, "My mother is the most beautiful woman in the world." Finally she finds her mother, who is described as an ordinary-looking woman. After the reading, Lori commented, "What is beautiful to one person may not be beautiful to another. My mother thinks I am pretty."

Because Lori's comments and writing indicated that she was able to recognize and identify the motivations of fairy-tale characters, Mrs. S decided to introduce her to realistic fiction about children with disabilities. She hoped that reading about people who were solving their problems might help Lori find the courage to try to meet the other children halfway. Mrs. S started with *Angie and Me*, Rebecca Jones' story about Jenna, a girl with a physical disability who feels rejected by her school friends. When Jenna goes to go to a hospital for treatment, however, she finds that she makes friends easily with the children there. Lori's journal entry indicated that she identified with Jenna:

> Jenna made good friends in the hospital. Those kids treated her like any other person. They did not think they were different from Jenna, like the kids in her school.
> That is what is hard. People have different handicaps, but they still have feelings.

Sorrow's Song by Larry Callen is the story of a girl who is unable to speak. The girl is isolated and lonely and has no one to play with. One day, she finds an injured whooping crane, but overhears a group of hunters making plans to capture and kill the bird. Fortunately, she is able to communicate with another child who agrees to help her save the crane. The two girls free the crane and, in the process, become good friends.

In response to this story, Lori told Mrs. S: "*Sorrow's Song* makes me feel happy. The girl in the story was sad 'cause she had no friends. She could not even talk. But her friend could understand her. The girl found out that she did not need to talk to get a friend."

Jay Slepian's *The Alfred Summer* portrays the developing friendship among four children as they try to help Alfred build a boat in the basement of his apartment house. All the characters have a special need of some kind—but all discover they have something to offer the group. For example, Lester, the narrator, who is unhappy because his physical disability limits what he can do, finds that he can contribute by helping his mentally handicapped friend.

After reading the book twice, Lori wrote in her journal:

> Lester did not think he could do anything. His mother worried about him too much. Alfred could not even use a boat. He lived in the city. But that didn't matter. Those kids helped each other. Lester was the best helper and made the other kids feel good about themselves.

This kind of realistic fiction reflected Lori's own feelings and experiences and helped her realize that problems can be overcome. As the school year progressed, she began taking some tentative steps toward establishing relationships with other children, and they, in turn, began to relate to her. Although she still needed encouragement, Lori no longer automatically expected to be rejected. She told Mrs. S: "Maybe I thought no one wanted to be my friend, so I didn't give anyone a chance. Maybe they thought I didn't like them."

Just as telling was the change in attitude among Lori's classmates. While the prejudices of some children never disappeared entirely, they certainly lost their power to prevent Lori from being accepted as a member of the class.

Overcoming Stereotypes: Stanley's Story

Because none of the children in Stanley's class had ever met someone who was visually impaired, they were both curious and fearful.

At the beginning of the school year, the itinerant teacher for the visually impaired visited the class to talk about blindness and visual impairments. She wanted to help the children understand the difficulties Stanley faced and show them that children with visual impairments are able to learn. She displayed the special equipment Stanley would be using and gave each child a copy of the Braille alphabet. At her suggestion, the children enthusiastically agreed to try eating lunch wearing blindfolds.

To give blindness a human face, this teacher then related a Chinese fable called *The First Storyteller*, the story of a blind prince. When this prince was very small, his father, the king, decided that he was unsuitable to inherit the throne and ordered a servant to take him to the forest and abandon him.

Fortunately, the animals who lived in the forest found the little boy and made him a home. They fed him and told him stories. The prince learned their language and listened eagerly to their stories.

When he grew up, the prince decided to leave the forest and live among people. Traveling from village to village, he learned the language of people and related the fascinating stories the animals had told him. The people told him stories, too. Gradually, word of the blind storyteller and his wonderful stories began to spread far and wide.

Hearing about the storyteller, the king ordered him brought to the palace. When the king saw him, he realized that the talented young man was his son and begged him to return to the palace, promising that someday he would be king. The storyteller refused, saying, "Please, Father, do not make me live in the palace. I would have nothing to do. I would feel like a prisoner. I want to be free and live among the people."

With that, the blind prince left the palace and lived a long and happy life sharing stories with people.

After hearing this tale, the children asked many revealing questions: "If you are blind, do you hear better?" "If a blind person were king, how would he know how his country looks?" "Did someone help the storyteller travel from village to village?" "How did the storyteller know people were listening?" "How does Stanley know which of us is talking to him?"

Noting that some of the questions embarrassed Stanley, Ms Y, his classroom teacher, resolved to use literature to help overcome the children's stereotypes about blindness and blind people. She selected carefully, however, avoiding stories that depicted blind or visually impaired characters as overly brave or heroic. Stories like these simply promote a different kind of stereotyping. Some of the stories she found effective were:

— *A Cane in Her Hand* by Ada B. Litchfield, which relates the story of a girl who learned to accept her blindness.
— *Cakes and Miracles* by Barbara Diamond Goldin, about a blind boy who showed his mother that he could bake cookies like other children.
— *Carver* by Ruth Yaffe Radin, the story of a blind boy who wanted to be a carver like his father.
— *A Story of Jean* by Susan Gaitskell, a biography of well-known children's writer Jean Little, which relates how Little overcame the teasing of other children.

All these books portray blind children as ordinary youngsters who have their own ideas, hopes and dreams.

Ms Y found that humorous stories were particularly helpful in relieving tensions and encouraging realistic perceptions. For example, *The Spectacles* by Eileen Raskin helped Stanley overcome his self-consciousness about wearing goggles. In this story, a girl who needed eyeglasses found the world very confusing. She thought the mail carrier was a fire-eating dragon and her doctor was a blue elephant. When she got her eye glasses, though, the world was no longer so confusing.

After listening to the stories like these, Stanley's classmates became more comfortable with him and began asking him questions about his sight problems: "If you're blind, how do you know what you're eating?" "Do you feel scared because you can't see good?" "Do you watch television?"

Stanley patiently answered the questions, even when he clearly thought they were silly, a process that helped increase his own understanding of his classmates' attitudes.

The children's journal entries demonstrated their new understanding:

> Stanley is called blind, but he is not blind. He can see a little. He belongs here and we are his buddies. It is like we are all one big family and Stanley is one of us.

> I think Stanley can learn things from us and we can learn things from him.

> Stanley should be in our class because there is no reason why he shouldn't. I think he is as smart as us.

> I think Stanley should be in this class because he is no different from us. Stanley is only part blind. He knows how to use the computer.

Solving Personal Problems: Harvey's Story

Mr. C, Harvey's teacher, knew the little boy before his accident and could not help but feel sorry for him. Like Harvey's parents, who were determined to make their son's life as normal as possible, Mr. C realized that this boy had been through a traumatic change and needed time to accept his disabilities and rebuild his confidence and sense of worth.

When Mr. C read Kenneth Grahame's *The Wind in the Willows* to the class, he encouraged the children to write about the characters in their journals. Working with a computer and an expanded keyboard, Harvey wrote:

Mole likes to get out of his hole. He likes to feel free. I feel like Mole. Toad is lonely. He always has to do something to get attention. Toad gets himself in trouble cause he feels lonely.

When invited to follow up by composing a letter to one of the characters, Harvey wrote to Toad:

Dear Toad,
I know you are not happy. You want your friends to like you. You should not be silly. You think your friends do not care about you. Your friends worry about you. My friends worry about me. You should show your friends that you care about them too.

After hearing Mr. C read aloud *The Wizard Of Oz* by L. Frank Baum, Harvey wrote:

If I could be like anyone, I would like to be like the Cowardly Lion. He wanted to be brave. He found out that you only have to act brave to be brave. The lion felt scared a lot of the time. That is why he needed to be brave.

Mr. C then decided to read aloud a story about a child with a disability and selected *Nick Joins In* by Joe Lasker. A physically disabled boy who uses a wheelchair, Nick is sad and lonely because he cannot play ball with his friends. He becomes a hero, however, when he solves a problem on the playing field.

Clearly moved by Nick's story, Harvey told Mr. C: "Nick was sad like me. He could not run and play ball with other kids. He showed the other kids he was not helpless. He saved the game for them. Kids like me are not helpless."

Encouraged by Harvey's response, Mr. C then read Ron Roy's *Move Over, Wheelchairs Coming Through,* which describes the adventures of children with physical disabilities who engage in sports and other activities. This book helped Harvey think differently about himself and his future as he realized that his opportunities to participate in sports weren't completely cut off. Mr. C observed a change in Harvey's outlook as he seemed to develop more patience with himself and become more cooperative with those who wanted to help him.

When Mr. C read *Jim Abbott, Star Pitcher* by Bill Gutman, Harvey told him: "Maybe I can be like Jim Abbott. He had only one hand. He didn't let that keep him from being a star baseball player." Harvey wrote about being independent:

Being independent means you learn to do things for yourself. I know I do some things better than others. And I can ask my friends to do things for me that I can't do. I can do some things for them too.

Choosing Literature about Children with Disabilities

Mental handicaps, blindness, deafness, physical disabilities, and learning and emotional problems are difficult for young children to understand, and portraying fictional characters with special needs in ways that enable young children to relate to them presents a challenge to writers. When selecting books about children with disabilities, teachers need to apply the same criteria as they would when choosing any literature for the class. Is the language appropriate? Are the characters well-developed? Is the story engaging? At the same time, it's important to be sensitive to the special issues involved in presenting literature about children with disabilities. If books are chosen carefully and thoughtfully, they can promote understanding by providing information and challenging mistaken ideas and stereotypes about people with disabilities.

In *Disability in Modern Children's Fiction*, John Quicke wrote:

"It is a convention that writing for children must have a happy ending in one way or another, so that the child reader is not left in the air, so to speak, having to grapple on his or her own with negative emotions and dark thoughts. In some books this happy ending seems too contrived. It is not a credible development of the story line or a way to end the book which is faithful to the characters involved."

The way characters are described is important. For example, in *Welcome Home, Jellybean*, Marlene Fanta Shyer describes a mentally handicapped girl without making her seem too different. Although Fanta Shyer says the girl sometimes looks "funny," she adds that when her hair is combed, "she looks pretty much like every other kid." This kind of description emphasizes the child rather than the mental handicap.

84

In addition, it's important to look for books in which the behavior of the disabled character reflects the behavior of a child with a particular disability without exaggeration or stereotyping. *We Laugh, We Love, We Cry: Children Living with Mental Retardation* by Thomas Bergman and *My Friend Leslie* by Maxine Rosenberg, for example, present realistic portrayals of children with mental handicaps by showing children who make friends and engage in activities with other children.

Books showing that the lives of people with disabilities do not revolve around their disabilities and that their families do not live in isolation foster realistic expectations. When they matter-of-factly portray disabled characters who are participating in activities with their non-disabled peers, these books help create expectations of inclusion.

As with any reading experience, it's important for teachers to share their own responses to books about disabled children and make their thoughts and feelings known. And in the same way that activities like writing about book characters, discussions, creative drama and so on inspire children to engage in experiences with any literature, these activities also encourage them to engage in experiences with books about children with disabilities.

Lori, Stanley and Harvey—Finding Acceptance

There is no substitute for literature in helping children share feelings and experiences. Nor is there a better way to foster independent reading.

For Lori, Stanley and Harvey, books provided a bridge to understanding. By carefully selecting literature that realistically portrayed children with disabilities, their teachers created an atmosphere that fostered self- and social acceptance and helped the children relate to one another. Literature helped dispel the fears and stereotypes that often surround children with disabilities and ensured that Lori, Stanley and Harvey would be accepted as contributing members of their classroom communities.

. . . .

INCLUDING CHILDREN

WHO CANNOT SPEAK

"When mother was busy I worked by myself, trying to make out new words whenever I came across them. I used to try and spell out the names of objects around me at home, like fire, picture, dog, door, chair, and so on. I was very proud of myself when I had mastered a new word and could write it down for mother to show her what a great scholar I was."

Christy Brown
My Left Foot

Cindy is a bright and friendly six-year-old who has a severe form of cerebral palsy and is unable to walk or talk. Her vision is impaired and she has only limited use of her arms and hands. Despite the unintelligibility of her speech, her parents have never doubted her ability to understand language. Cindy participates in family, community and church events and attends the neighborhood school where a classroom aide helps her with eating, toileting and other activities. Cindy loves listening to stories and uses a laptop computer with a speech synthesizer to interact with her classmates.

Eight-year-old Jane is an enthusiastic reader who enjoys interacting with other children. She was born with Krouzon's syndrome, a rare genetic condition that can include facial malformations such as a cleft palate and a deformed jaw. The malformation of Jane's mouth and jaw makes speech impossible. Although her vision is impaired, she is able to see well enough to read and write. In fact, Jane taught herself to read and write, inventing her own system of communication that involved writing abbreviated notes to her mother to make requests or state opinions. For example, when she wanted a new dress, she wrote a note that said, "Too small clothes. Buy new."

Seven-year-old Eddy has Down's syndrome. Although his language development is delayed and his speech is inarticulate, Eddy has learned to indicate his needs, wants and interests by gesturing, grunting and smiling. He is a friendly child who is interested in the other children in his classroom and eager to participate in games and classroom activities. Unable to read or write, he nevertheless enjoys looking at the illustrations in picture books.

Ensuring that children with severe disabilities are accepted and included in classroom activities presents a special challenge. Although these children require the intervention of special educators, speech-and-language clinicians, parents, therapists and aides, the opportunities to learn are created by their classroom teachers.

When children begin to speak, they learn the pragmatic functions of language—that words and phrases can be used to influence and regulate the actions of other people. Children who are unable to speak rely on facial expressions, body postures, eye contact, vocal sounds and hand movements to express interest and desire. While these behaviors may enable them to communicate their feelings, they are not a substitute for a language system, especially when it comes to expressing ideas. Nevertheless, the inability to speak should never be interpreted as an inability to understand language. Although it is impossible to speak without understanding language, it is possible to be unable to speak and still have a perfect understanding of language. Unless they have auditory or hearing problems, non-speaking children are listening and acquiring an appreciation of the language they hear.

Furthermore, augmentative systems of communication give non-speaking children a voice. For many of these children, augmentative systems are the route to literacy.

Speech and Language Disorders

Speech disorder is an umbrella term used to refer to difficulties in producing intelligible speech, while language disorder refers to difficulties perceiving and comprehending complex language patterns. Both speech and language disorders are frequently associated with cerebral palsy and other neurological conditions.

Two specific speech disorders are frequently associated with cerebral palsy. Dysarthria, which results from an inability to control the muscles involved in producing speech, prevents the articulation of intelligible speech sounds. Dyspraxia refers to the inability to perform in sequence the intricate movements of the mouth and tongue required to produce speech. On its own, neither dysarthria or dyspraxia interferes with the ability to comprehend language. Many children with these disorders are able to learn to read and write.

Stuttering, stammering, lisping and voice problems are other speech disorders. Although children with these disorders don't usually have any difficulty comprehending language, they can feel frustrated and isolated.

Because language disorders interfere with the ability to understand both oral and written language, children with these disorders have trouble both producing and comprehending language. These auditory discrimination problems affect both the rate and comprehension of complex speech. Affected children are easily distracted by extraneous noise and have trouble paying attention to speech sounds. Some children have difficulty distinguishing speech sounds from environmental noise. Speaking slowly and directly to these children often helps them maintain their attention. This is particularly true of children who have language processing difficulties.

David Koppenhaver and David Yoder studied the reading and writing problems of children with severe speech and physical disabilities. Although these children typically make more errors than others, their errors are not different in kind. Koppenhaver and Yoder also reported that the inability to type quickly, visual problems and fatigue impose additional limitations on these children and noted that working with language and formulating sentences are essential for children whose opportunities to use language are limited.

Augmentative Systems of Communication

Augmentative systems of communication provide non-speaking children with opportunities to use language to communicate with other people. Doreen Blischak, a specialist in augmentative communication, worked with nine-year-old

Thomas, who has quadriplegic cerebral palsy, a visual impairment and dysarthria. In an article in *Language, Speech and Hearing Services in Schools*, Blischak described Thomas's dependence on his ability to communicate using a laptop computer:

> "It is intriguing to consider that although communication competency can be quite difficult to achieve for individuals with impairments as severe as Thomas's, in reality, he is quite dependent on effective communication to overcome his physical and visual limitations. Thomas relies heavily on his language and literacy skills for social contact, to learn about his world, and to actively participate in life around him. Communication is his key to independence and participation in the world around him."

For children who cannot speak, augmentative communication is the only means of using language to communicate. A variety of systems is available, ranging from non-electronic, portable communication aids to highly sophisticated computer-based speaking and writing systems. Many of them can be used interchangeably.

Simple systems depend on words or pictures to convey a variety of messages. The simplest may consist of a sheet of cardboard on which pictures, photographs, objects, symbols, or words or phrases are shown. The child points to or looks at a picture or other symbol to make a choice or reply to a question. While these communication boards may be effective in some situations, their uses are limited and most children require more comprehensive systems to enable them to participate fully in classroom interactions.

Comprehensive augmentative systems help children perform a broad range of communicative functions with various partners in a variety of environments. Comprehensive computer-based systems enable users to express themselves—construct sentences, express thoughts and ideas, seek information, and make demands and requests—in a variety of situations. Even young children can be taught to use these systems, which can be tailored to the children's specific needs.

Instead of the standard computer keyboard, augmentative systems often include switches that can be operated with the hand or head. Or the keyboard may be adapted to alter the size, location and sensitivity of the keys. Expanded keyboards with touch-sensitive screens that include pictures, letters and punctuation can make it possible for children who have limited use of their hands to use computers.

In addition, speech output devices can convert printed text into spoken messages. Speech synthesizers can be used with standard computer keyboards and monitors or combined with a transparent touch screen that is mounted on a standard computer monitor.

Remote pointing systems, which consist of a pointing device that directs a light beam or infrared signal at an array of items displayed on the computer screen, are also available. The pointing device may be mounted on different parts of the body, such the hand, arm, leg or head.

Software that reproduces speech synthetically helps severely disabled children gain experience using language in a variety of ways. For example, children who are unable to turn the pages of a book can read stories presented on a computer screen and turn the pages by pushing a switch or key. A list of some of the programs currently available is included in the reference material that concludes this book.

The special programs provided by speech-and-language clinicians, special educators and aides are adjuncts to, not substitutes for, participation in classroom activities. The social setting of the classroom offers rich opportunities to develop and practice skills.

Learning to Read and Write: Cindy's Story

Cindy's severe form of cerebral palsy has affected her ability to walk, talk and see. In fact, her ability to hear is her only unimpaired channel of learning.

The district itinerant teacher for the visually impaired and a speech-and-language clinician work with Cindy in the classroom. Cindy enjoys storytimes and often listens to taped books when the other children are reading and looking at books. At first, she used an electronic board with two buttons to indicate Yes and No answers to questions.

Because her ability to move her hands and arms is limited, Cindy is unable to use the Braille alphabet. Yet her teachers believed that she needed to experience a form of written language. As a result, they decided to use the Fishburne alphabet, shown here, to introduce her to letters and words. This tactile system, which is produced on one-inch strips of heavy plastic tape with a hand-held printer, uses dots and dashes to represent the letters of the alphabet. Their size and configuration makes them easy to identify.

Morse Code for the Computer

a	. _		p	. _ _ .
b	_ . . .		q	_ _ . _
c	_ . .		r	. _ .
d	_		s	. . .
e	.		t	_
f	. . _ .		u	. . _
g	_ _ .		v	... _
h	. . . .		w	. _ _
i	. .		x	_ . . _
j	. _ _ _		y	_ . _
k	_ . _		z	_ _ . .
l	._ . .		space	.. _ _
m	_ _		period	. _ . _
n	_ .		comma	_ _ . . _ _
o	_ _ _		question	. . _ _ . .

Mr. L, the itinerant teacher, used the Fishburne alphabet to make Cindy an alphabet book and several storybooks. This was useful in showing Cindy that letters have shapes and can be arranged to form words. But it is a time-consuming method of producing books and gave Cindy no opportunity to explore books independently.

Once Cindy had learned the alphabet and acquired a reading vocabulary of some 30 words, her teachers began to investigate more sophisticated systems. A special education technologist provided Cindy with a computer equipped with a switch that enabled her to express herself by spelling out words in Morse code. A speech synthesizer translated into speech the text Cindy entered.

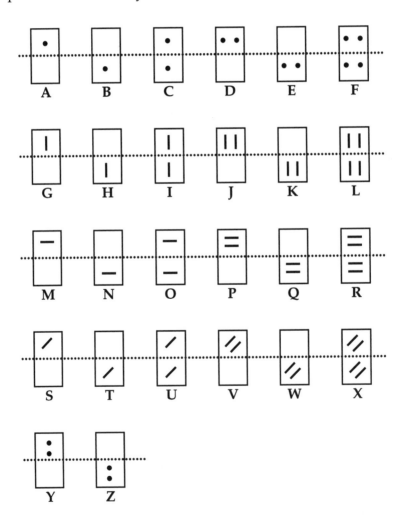

Although Cindy's computer was equipped with a single switch, systems that use two switches are also available—the left switch enters the dots and the right enters the dashes. Cindy's computer included a Morse code-based word-processing program, which enabled her to indicate choices, formulate sentences, spell words and initiate conversations with other children. This "talking" computer gave Cindy a voice in the classroom and the written work she produced reflected her growing mastery of language:

> I am a girl who likes to play. I like to pretend. When I talk
> to other children with my machine voice. They hear me
> and know what I say. The machine does not talk for me.
> I tell it what to say. It is me talking.

With the voice provided by the computer, Cindy was able to read, write and participate in classroom activities. Her teachers were delighted with her progress. She operated her tape recorder and was able to choose the taped books she wanted to listen to. In addition, she wrote book reports, stories and poems.

> I like to talk. I like to play.
> I talk and play every day.
> I talk to my friends and they talk to me.
> And that is the way I like it to be.

It is extremely difficult if not impossible to assess the language abilities of children whose speech is unintelligible until they have access to a mode of communication. Cindy's remarkable progress indicated how easily talent and ability can be obscured by multiple disabilities. Although her parents had always believed that she was bright and interested, even they were surprised at how quickly she progressed.

Learning to Use Language: Jane's Story

Although she could not speak, Jane's vision problem did not prevent her from reading print, interpreting pictures and writing legibly. The brief, abbreviated messages she wrote using a felt pen or pencil, however, gave her little experience formulating sentences.

Before she arrived in Mrs. F's primary classroom, Jane had attended a special program for children with developmental disabilities. The teacher there had urged Jane's parents to enroll her in the neighborhood school, pointing out that the pace of instruction in the special program was too slow for Jane. A mainstream classroom, the teacher said, would offer their daughter many more opportunities to develop her language and literacy skills. Fearing that Jane would be teased and rejected by the other children, her parents resisted at first, but the teacher was persuasive and they finally agreed to the transfer.

When she entered the neighborhood school, a speech-and-language clinician gave Jane a series of tests that showed that her vocabulary was commensurate with her age and that her ability to comprehend language was far greater than her ability to produce grammatical sentences. Although Jane did not formulate complete sentences, the phrases she used included adjectives, pronouns, prepositions, adverbs and a variety of verb forms. For example, to ask questions, she relied on her own system, which involved placing a question mark before a written phrase (e.g., ? Go play now).

Jane could answer tag questions, such as "You liked this story, didn't you?" but she had difficulty with Who, What, Where and Why questions.

In the special program, Jane had learned to communicate using Blissymbolics and a communication board. A symbol system originally invented by Charles Bliss to serve as an international language, the Bliss system uses pictographs and logographs to represent the parts of speech. These are combined to enable users to communicate in complete sentences. Today, the symbols are most widely used among children and adults with severe speech impairments. Some of the symbols are illustrated on the following page.

When Jane first entered Mrs. F's classroom, she was given a Touch Talker, a portable electronic speech device that she could use independently, making it far more efficient than a communication board. By pressing on the overlay of Bliss symbols on the touch-sensitive screen, Jane was able to ask and answer questions. The pre-programmed messages were easily adapted to specific activities in the classroom.

Although the Touch Talker was helpful, Jane needed a more comprehensive system that would enable her to formulate sentences and produce her own messages rather than relying on the pre-programmed messages available on the Touch Talker. While she waited to be assessed by the special education technologist, Jane communicated with Mrs. F by writing notes. Here's a transcript of one of their conversations:

Mrs. F: Do you have favorite stories?
Jane: Like all stories.
Mrs. F: Do you like fairy stories?
Jane: Best.
Mrs. F: You went horseback riding. Do you like it?
Jane: It fun.
Mrs. F: Do you like swimming?
Jane: Do backstroke. Walk in water.

Jane also wrote notes to the other children—Spell name, Sit next you, Play outside, Raining now. Although some of the children avoided Jane, many responded to her warmth and humor. She was friendly, interested and responsive.

Bliss symbols can resemble the things they represent.

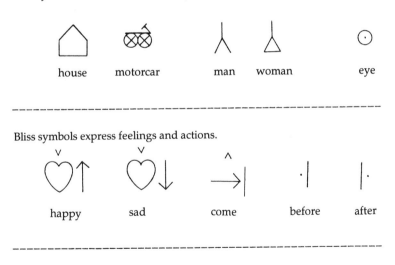

| house | motorcar | man | woman | eye |

Bliss symbols express feelings and actions.

| happy | sad | come | before | after |

The symbols represent several meanings.

beautiful, lovely
pretty, cute

make believe, pretend,
magic

The computer system designed for Jane included a speech synthesizer, a screen on which the print size and contrast could be adjusted, and an adapted keyboard with large print. As Jane worked with the speech-and-language clinician to develop her understanding of syntax and sentence patterns, the written work she produced on the computer began to reflect her growing ability to produce sentences. Here's what Jane wrote in response to the story *The Red Shoes*:

This girl got magic shoes. They red. She wear them and she dance and dance. She tired and shoes do not stop dancing. The girl get trouble. She not do what she want. She do what shoes want. Some people wish things not good for them.

Jane also began to create her own stories and revise them with the other children, such as this one about a magic mouse.

This story tells about a magic mouse. He make himself big like giant or small like bug. He like to be big. His friends did not like his magic. They not know when he get bigger or smaller. He change too much. Friends like you stay same so they know you better. I do not want my friends to change.

Initially, Mrs. F was concerned about how Jane would be received by the other children, but she soon discovered that Jane could solve her own problems. She put other children at ease and did not hesitate to compliment or thank them when they tried to help her. Mrs. F wrote this letter to her parents:

When Jane was first enrolled in my class, I must admit I was uneasy. I knew so little about teaching children with disabilities like Jane's. And like you, I was worried about how the other children would react to her. I soon discovered that I worried needlessly. Jane is teaching us all about learning. No matter how difficult Jane finds a task, she does not let herself get discouraged. She keeps on trying and is always ready for a challenge. As one of the children said, "Jane brings a lot of happy to this room." I think so too.

Eddy's speech was so difficult to understand that Ms N couldn't decide whether he was using language or just making sounds. As a result, she had no idea of what to expect from him. On the recommendation of the speech-and-language clinician, Eddy was given a picture board that included four pictures indicating lunch and snack, toilet, playtime and storytime. Eddy pointed to the pictures on the board before and after these activities.

A classroom aide made additional picture boards that included the names of the objects shown in the pictures. In fact, Eddy was introduced to his classmates using a picture board.

Hello. My name is Eddy (photograph of Eddy).
My favorite food is ice cream (picture of an ice cream cone).
I have a brother named Sam (photo of Sam).
I like to come to school (photo of school).

Because Eddy clearly recognized the photographs, the school's resource teacher decided a visual approach to literacy made sense and selected The Bridge Reading Program by Alison Dewsbury, Jennifer Jennings and David Boyle. This uses logographs or pictures labeled with words and simple phrases.

So that Eddy could make requests and answer questions in the classroom, the resource teacher made a communication board with logographs from the Bridge series. When Ms N read *The Three Little Pigs* to the class, the resource teacher made Eddy his own simplified version using eight different picture symbols. And she used the same symbols to make word and picture cards so Eddy could tell about the story. The cards were inserted in clear plastic pockets on his picture board.

To give Eddy an opportunity to request a book to be read aloud, Ms N encouraged him to bring books from home. One morning he brought in Seymour Reit's *The Rebus Bears*, which uses rebuses to tell a simplified version of *The Three Bears*.

Noticing that Eddy was smiling as she read the book and pointed to the signs, Ms N realized that familiarity with a particular book helped Eddy follow the story. Repeated readings of the same book help children with language disorders anticipate story events and hear the language. This was borne out when the classroom aide re-read to Eddy the stories Ms N read at storytime. His comprehension seemed better when she read these stories slowly and emphasized the rhythms of language. In fact, as the weeks passed, Ms N noticed that he was becoming much more attentive and aware of language.

The aide also helped Eddy work with rhymes, trace letters and recognize words. As she and Eddy worked through each of the five levels of the Bridge Reading Program, she devised simple matching games with words and logographs. Eddy worked slowly and carefully and was able to answer questions by pointing to logographs on his communication board. The aide was pleased when the other children joined him in playing some of the games she devised. The day Eddy pointed to a word instead of the logograph, his teachers knew he was progressing.

Eddy also began working independently on a computer operated with a simple switch. A software program that featured animated cartoon characters helped him work on letter-recognition. This interactive program was highly motivating and Eddy indicated his pleasure at working on the computer. Eventually, Eddy acquired a reading vocabulary of more than 50 words.

When Ms N wrote a report to Eddy's parents, she noted the power of motivation in overcoming obstacles. She also realized how few opportunities children like Eddy have to experience success unless someone else makes it possible. Her report said:

> I realize how much Eddy's motivation is shaped by success. Few of us are willing to try things if we are convinced we will fail. As I have observed Eddy over the past few months, I can see how motivated he has become.
>
> Eddy is working hard and I know how much he wants to read. No one can predict how far he will progress with reading and writing, but I am certain that no limitations should be placed on his opportunities to learn.

Cindy, Jane and Eddy—Joining the Classroom Community

Undismayed by the severity of their disabilities, Cindy's, Jane's and Eddy's teachers focused on their abilities and ensured that they had opportunities to participate actively in mainstream classroom literacy activities. With the support of teachers who believe in their abilities, excite their interest, and guide their efforts, it's clear that even children who are unable to speak can learn to read and write.

INCLUDING CHILDREN

WITH SPECIAL NEEDS

"Full inclusion occurs when a child with a disability learns in a general education classroom alongside his or her agemates with all the necessary supports. These supports are provided through extensive teamwork and communication."

Ray Van Dyke, Martha Ann Stallings and Kenna Colley
In *Phi Delta Kappan*

The terms "mainstreaming," "integration" and "inclusion" describe policies of educating children with special needs in their neighborhood schools. Inclusion is not a new idea. In *Exceptional Children*, Burton Blatt reported that Alexander Graham Bell wrote in 1900:

"Believing as I do, in the policy of decentralization, in dealing with defective children—the policy of separating them from one another, as much as practicable during the process of education, and keeping them in constant personal contact with their friends and relatives and ordinary normal people—I would say that it would be better to send teachers to these children, rather than send children to the teachers."

There are many reasons for including disabled children in mainstream schools. A mainstream primary classroom provides far richer language and learning experiences than are possible in segregated environments, which cut children off from normal childhood experiences and do not prepare them for living in the real world. Segregation in school leads to segregation in life. Children with disabilities have the right to be part of mainstream society.

It's in the primary classroom that children make important discoveries about themselves and about learning. The policy of inclusion is meaningless without the involvement and participation of classroom teachers who can make inclusion a rich and rewarding experience and integration a reality. Although specialist itinerant or resource teachers may see the child every day, it is the classroom teacher who creates the opportunities that transform the philosophy of inclusion into daily practice. Working with special educators, classroom aides, and therapists requires advanced planning and consultation.

COLLABORATION WITH SPECIAL EDUCATORS, THERAPISTS AND AIDES

Inclusion practices involve classroom teachers in new relationships with a variety of people—special education teachers, therapists, classroom aides and parents. Working relationships take time to develop, however, and require a clear definition of the roles and responsibilities of everyone involved. Teachers benefit by being actively involved so that they feel comfortable asking questions and seeking advice.

Special Educators and Consultants

Although the terms used to describe special educators vary from school district to district, they may include resource and itinerant teachers and consultants. In some districts, special educators are based in a single school; in others, they act as consultants for all the schools in a particular district. The services available depend in large part on the size of the school district.

Resource teachers or, as they are sometimes called, integration teachers provide consultation, learning materials and individualized programs to children and their teachers. In small districts, a single resource teacher may serve an entire school district. In urban centers, each school may have its own resource teacher.

Specialist teachers who travel from school to school to work with children with vision or hearing problems are called itinerant teachers. When working with visually impaired children, these teachers may teach Braille literacy, provide specialized instruction and equipment, adapt classroom materials, provide books in Braille or large print and teach computer skills. They may also provide instruction in life skills and travel training for students with severe sight problems. This training may involve, for example, learning to use a white cane to identify obstacles, negotiate stairs and narrow spaces, and move with confidence in the school and the community. Smaller school districts may share the services of one itinerant teacher.

Itinerant teachers for the hearing impaired provide individualized instruction, learning materials, equipment and language enrichment activities. They are proficient in both sign language and oral methods of working with children whose hearing is impaired. These teachers consult with audiologists and speech-and-language clinicians and provide devices to facilitate listening in the classroom.

Special education technologists assess children's computer needs and provide advice and guidance to teachers. They help teachers select the most appropriate software programs and equipment for individual students.

Aides and child development workers are paraprofessionals who assist teachers in the classroom. Working with the guidance of classroom teachers, special educators, speech-and-language clinicians, physical or occupational therapists and child psychologists or psychiatrists, their specific duties are usually determined by the needs of the specific child. They may help with feeding, toileting or ensuring that the children are able to participate in classroom activities.

Planning for Inclusion

Opportunities for growth are created when teachers base their planning on children's abilities—not their disabilities. Personality, motivation, previous experience and familiarity with books and print are as varied among children with disabilities as they are among their non-disabled peers. There are no clear boundaries between normal and abnormal development.

Disabilities affect the way things are learned rather than what needs to be learned. Like all children, children with special needs tend to live up to the expectations of the adults in their lives. Inclusion practices are based on the following guidelines:

— Children with special needs are more like their non-disabled peers than they are different from them.

— The aims of literacy instruction apply to all children.
— Children with special needs are expected to abide by the same rules and regulations as other children. Too many special concessions teach children to feel different and their peers to become less tolerant.
— Knowledge of the special methods, materials and equipment that are available for children with special needs helps teachers develop realistic plans.
— Program adaptations are governed by the needs of the individual child. They may vary from simple modifications to the use of highly specialized materials and equipment.
— Students should be encouraged to take responsibility for their own work and behavior. Do not make excuses or exceptions.
— Teachers need to be aware of the limitations of the learning materials and technology available to disabled children.
— The choices of children who refuse to use a particular aid must be respected. Discuss the child's preferences with the resource teacher or parent.
— Topics dealing with inclusion and other disability issues should be incorporated in workshops, conferences and professional development programs.
— No more than one or two children with disabilities should be integrated into a mainstream primary classroom at any one time to avoid giving children with special needs too high a profile.
— Children using Braille and other adapted materials need ample work space. Desks and storage places should be designed to make materials and equipment readily available. Well-organized work spaces help avoid confusion and frustration. Desks should be uncluttered.

It's important to emphasize that the context of the classroom is the framework within which individualized programs and adaptations take place. This means that programs for children with special needs are grounded in the classroom teacher's preferred methodology and teaching strategies.

Assessment

The same methods that teachers use to assess the progress of non-disabled children can be applied to the child with special needs. One of the most valuable tools is the time teachers spend talking to and observing children reading and writing. Observational records are especially useful in determining the type of additional support an individual child may need. Pupil-teacher interviews and conferences are opportunities to discover the learning strategies a particular child is using as well as his or her level of comprehension.

To plan efficiently, teachers need information about children's backgrounds, previous experiences with books and stories, and interests and motivation. Here are some questions that can help guide the information-gathering and observation processes:

— Does the child have opportunities to hear stories read at home?
— How does the child indicate comprehension?
— Does the child look at books independently?
— Does the child enjoy listening to stories?
— Does the child have favorite books?
— Does the child show interest in selecting books?
— Can the child make predictions?
— Does the child relate reading to his or her own experiences?
— Does the child make use of background information?
— Can the child use picture clues?
— Can the child place story events in sequence?
— Can the child use context clues to decode words?
— Does the child make use of opportunities to read in the classroom?
— Can the child read for sustained periods?
— Does the child select a range of reading materials?
— Does the child have access to a variety of materials?
— Does the child have opportunities for independent practice?
— Can the child identify characters, settings and problems?
— Can the child classify books into fiction and non-fiction?
— Does the child respond to groupwork?

- Does the child who is having difficulties show a pattern of miscues?
- Is the child overly dependent on one particular strategy?
- Are the child's difficulties reflected in other aspects of the curriculum?

As with all children, the attitudes, expectations and motivation of children with special needs power the drive to learn to read and write. Because self-evaluation encourages children to take responsibility for their own learning, they benefit from charting their own progress. When they do this, they become actively involved in the process of learning to read and write. Dorothy Butler's granddaughter Cushla was never exposed to any method of direct reading instruction—unless providing her with language and story, in and out of books, can be called a method. In *Cushla and Her Books*, Butler said, "I believe it can, and that it is the best method of all. It produces children who experience reading as a joyous process, natural to the human state; children who absorb ideas as sponges absorb water."

Conclusion

Teachers are often unaware of how powerfully they affect children's lives. As Frank Smith noted in *Insult to Intelligence*, many authors, athletes, artists and other accomplished people attribute their success to a teacher who inspired or directed them to their life's work. If this is true, and I believe it is, imagine the influence of a teacher who believes in the capacity of a child with a disability to become an active and eager learner. Children flourish in the warming glow of a teacher's belief in their abilities.

Some children gradually outgrow their special needs as they become more skilled and self-confident. Others, especially those with physical disabilities, sensory impairments or more troublesome learning problems, continue to have special needs throughout their lives.

For all children, it is the classroom teacher who creates an atmosphere that fosters inclusion. In inclusive classrooms, all children learn to respect abilities and accept differences. In this environment, children with special needs learn to value what they share with other children and realize that their disabilities or special needs are not their most distinguishing characteristic.

Research and experience are demonstrating the many social and emotional values of inclusion. Anyone who doubts these, should meet children like those whose stories are told in this book, as well as the teachers who helped them learn to read and write.

. . . .

GLOSSARY

Definitions of diagnostic terms can be helpful in understanding the constraints and limitations imposed by disabilities. Keep in mind, however, that there may be wide variations among children who share a disability.

Behavioral and emotional disorders: Refer to disturbed social relationships with adults and peers. Emotional disorders range from mild to severe and include a variety of disturbed and disturbing behaviors, such as withdrawal, confusion, mood disorders, aggression and lack of involvement. Behavioral and emotional problems are associated with social and emotional deprivation. Pervasive disorders affect all aspects of a child's development.

Developmental disabilities: An inclusive term used to describe delayed cognitive, language, social and physical development. Children with developmental disabilities may also be physically disabled and experience communication and language problems. This diagnostic category includes children whose cognitive or language development is delayed, as well those with mental handicaps.

Hearing impairments: Vary from total deafness to mild hearing loss, though even a mild hearing loss can interfere with language acquisition. The term "deaf" refers to profound hearing loss. Children who are deaf require specialized language and communication interventions.

Language disorders: Refer to problems acquiring and using language. Immature speech patterns, frequent grammatical errors, and difficulty comprehending or following oral directions and recalling words may indicate a language disorder.

Learning disabilities: An umbrella term referring to a heterogeneous group of disorders that causes problems in acquiring reading, writing or mathematical skills. The disorders often cause a significant discrepancy between academic achievement and intellectual ability. Symptoms include difficulties interpreting written symbols, disorganization and confusion.

Learning disabilities may also be associated with problems focusing and maintaining attention. The term "attention deficit disorder" is often used to describe these difficulties. Environmental factors such as sound levels in the classroom may contribute to inattentiveness.

Mental handicaps: A general term describing delayed or impaired mental ability that can range from mild to severe. Cognitive problems may also be associated with deprivation in early learning experiences as well as social and environmental deprivation.

Physical disabilities: A general term used to describe the physical impairments caused by cerebral palsy, muscular dystrophy or other neurologically or physically disabling conditions. Cerebral palsy is a non-progressive condition caused by damage to the brain before, during or immediately after birth and may be associated with visual, language and speech problems. Other physical disabilities, such those caused by muscular dystrophy, may be progressive and have wide-ranging effects on a child's development. Closed head injuries and severe forms of infectious illnesses are other causes of physical disabilities.

Speech disorders: Describe difficulties producing articulate speech, including stuttering, articulation, lisps and voice problems. Many children with cerebral palsy have speech disorders resulting from an inability to control the muscles associated with speech.

Visual impairments: Vary from total blindness to near-normal vision. In Canada and the United States, the definition of visual impairment is based on visual acuity, a measure of the smallest image distinguishable by the eye. The term "blind" is used only to describe a severe impairment that makes it impossible for a child to use vision for learning.

. . . .

REFERENCES

Professional Literature

Barton, B. & D. Booth. *Stories in the Classroom: Storytelling, Reading Aloud and Role Playing with Children.* Markham, Ont.: Pembroke, 1990.

Bettelheim, B. *The Uses of Enchantment: The Meaning and Importance of Fairy Tales.* New York, N.Y.: Alfred A. Knopf, 1976.

Bigge, J. *Teaching Individuals with Physical and Multiple Disabilities* (3rd ed.). New York, N.Y.: Macmillan, 1991.

Blatt, B. "Friendly Letters on the Correspondence of Helen Keller, Anne Sullivan and Alexander Graham Bell." In *Exceptional Children.* Vol. 51, no. 5: 1985.

Blischak, D. "Thomas, the Writer: Case Study of a Child with Severe Physical, Speech and Visual Impairments. In *Language, Speech, and Hearing Services in Schools.* Vol. 26, no. 1: 1995.

Brown, C. *My Left Foot.* New York, N.Y.: Simon & Schuster, 1955.

Bryant, P.E., M. Bradley, H. MacLean & J. Crossland. "Nursery Rhymes, Phonological Skills, and Reading." In *Journal of Child Language.* Vol. 16, no. 2: 1989.

Butler, D. *Cushla and Her Books.* Auckland, New Zealand: Penguin, 1987.

Butler, D. *Five to Eight.* London, England: The Bodley Head, 1986.

Chall, J., V. Jacobs & L.E. Baldwin. *The Reading Crisis: Why Poor Children Fall Behind*. Cambridge, Mass.: Harvard University Press, 1990.

Chow, M., L. Dobson, M. Hurst & J. Nucich. *Whole Language: Practical Ideas*. Scarborough, Ont.: Pippin Publishing, 1991.

Chukovsky, K. *From Two to Five*. Berkeley, Calif.: University of California Press, 1968.

Goswami, U. & P. Bryant. *Phonological Skills and Learning to Read*. East Sussex, England: Lawrence Erlbaum, 1990.

Graves M. "The Roles of Instruction in Fostering Vocabulary Development." In *The Nature of Vocabulary Acquisition*. (M.G. McKeown & M.E. Curtis, Eds.). Hillsdale, N.J.: Lawrence Erlbaum, 1987.

Halliday, M.A.K. *Learning How to Mean: Explorations in the Development of Language*. London, England: Edward Arnold, 1975.

Halliday, M.A.K. *Language As Social Semiotics: The Social Interpretation of Language and Meaning*. London, England: Edward Arnold, 1978.

Keller, H. *Teacher: Anne Sullivan Macy*. New York, N.Y.: Dolphin Books, 1955.

Kirshenblatt-Gimblett, B. "Children's Traditional Speech Play and Child Language." In *Speech Play: Research and Resources for Studying Linguistic Creativity*. (B. Kirshenblatt-Gimblett, Ed.). Philadelphia, Pa: University of Pennsylvania Press, 1976.

Koppenhaver, D.A. & D.E. Yoder. *Classroom Interaction, Literacy Acquisition, and Non-Speakng Children with Physical Impairments*. Paper presented at meeting of the International Society for Augmentative and Alternative Communication: Stockholm, Sweden, 1990.

Koppenhaver, D. & D.E. Yoder. "Literacy Issues in Persons with Severe Speech and Physical Impairments." In *Issues and Research in Special Education*. Vol. 2. (R. Gaylord-Ross, Ed.). New York, N.Y.: Teachers College Press, 1991.

Lederer, R. *The Play of Words: Fun and Games for Language Lovers*. New York, N.Y.: Simon & Schuster, 1990.

Lusseyran, J. *The Blind in Society and Blindness: A New Seeing of the World*. New York, N.Y.: The Myrin Institute, 1973.

Mangold, S. *The Mangold Developmental Program of Tactile Perception and Braille Letter Recognition*. Castro Valley, Calif.: Exceptional Teaching Aids, 1990.

McLane, J.B. & G.D. McNamee. *Early Literacy*. Cambridge, Mass.: Harvard University Press, 1990.

McNaughton, S. *Symbol Secrets*. Toronto, Ont.: Blissymbolics Communication Institute, 1975.

Nolan, C. *Under the Eye of the Clock: The Life Story of Christopher Nolan*. New York, N.Y.: St. Martin's Press, 1988.

Nolan, C. *Dam-Burst of Dreams*. Athens, Ohio: Ohio University Press, 1981.

Quicke, J. *Disability in Modern Children's Fiction*. London, England: Croom Helm, 1985.

Ralston, M. *An Exchange of Gifts: A Storyteller's Handbook*. Scarborough, Ont.: Pippin Publishing, 1990.

Raskin, R. & C. Ellison. *Parents, Kids and Computers*. New York, N.Y.: Random House, 1992.

Rubin, Z. *Children's Friendships*. Cambridge, Mass: Harvard University Press, 1980.

Smith, F. "Learning to Read: The Never-Ending Debate." In *Phi Delta Kappan*. Vol. 73, no. 6: 1992.

Smith, F. *Joining the Literacy Club*. Portsmouth, N.H.: Heinemann, 1988.

Smith, F. *Insult to Intelligence*. Portsmouth, N.H.: Heinemann, 1986.

Van Dyke, R., M.A. Stallings &K. Colley. "How to Build an Inclusive School Community." In *Phi Delta Kappan*. Vol. 76, no. 6: 1995.

Wells, G. *The Meaning-Makers: Children Learning Language and Using Language to Learn*. Portsmouth, N.H.: Heinemann, 1986.

Children's Books

Agee, J. *Go Hang a Salami! I'm a Lasagna Hog and Other Palindromes.* New York, N.Y.: Farrar, Straus & Giroux, 1991.

Ai-Ling L. *Yeh-Shen.* New York, N.Y.: Philomel Books, 1982.

Andersen, H.C. *Tales and Stories by Hans Christian Andersen.* Seattle, Wash.: University of Washington Press, 1980.

Baum, L.F. *The Wizard of Oz.* New York, N.Y.: Reilly & Lee, 1938.

Bemelmans, L. *Madeline.* New York, N.Y.: Simon & Schuster, 1939.

Brown, M.W. *Goodnight Moon.* New York, N.Y.: Harper and Row, 1947.

Brown, M.W. *Wait Till the Moon Is Full.* New York, N.Y.: Harper & Row, 1948.

Burnett, F.H. *The Secret Garden.* New York, N.Y.: J. B. Lipincott, 1962.

Dunn, S. with L. Pamenter. *Crackers and Crumbs: Chants for Whole Language.* Portsmouth, N.H.: Heinemann, 1989.

Edmonds, W. *The Puffin Book of Spelling Puzzles.* London, England: Penguin, 1992.

Grahame, K. *The Wind in the Willows.* New York, N.Y.: Viking, 1983.

Haviland, V. *Favorite Fairy Tales Told in Scotland.* Boston, Mass.: Little Brown, 1967.

Hubbell, P. *Catch Me a Wind.* Paterson, N.J.: Atheneum, 1958.

Lawson, R. *Rabbit Hill.* New York, N.Y.: Dell, 1976.

Lawson, R. *Ben and Me: A New and Astonishing Life of Benjamin Franklin as Written by His Good Mouse, Amos, Lately Discovered.* Boston, Mass.: Little Brown, 1939.

Lear, E. *A Was Once an Apple Pie.* Cambridge, Mass.: Candlewick Press, 1992.

McCloskey, R. *Make Way for Ducklings.* New York, N.Y.: Viking, 1966.

Piper, W. *The Little Engine That Could*. New York, N.Y.: Scholastic, 1961.

Rehyer, B. *My Mother Is the Most Beautiful Woman in the World*. New York, N.Y.: Lothrop, Lee & Shepard, 1945.

Reit, S. *The Rebus Bears*. New York, N.Y.: Bantam Doubleday Dell, 1989.

Rey, H.A. & M. Rey. *Curious George Visits the Zoo*. Boston, Mass.: Houghton Mifflin, 1966.

Sendak, M. *Where the Wild Things Are*. New York, N.Y.: Harper and Row, 1963.

Slobodkina, E. *Caps for Sale: A Tale of a Peddler, Some Monkeys and Their Monkey Business*. New York, N.Y.: Young Scott Books, 1947.

Terban, M. *Mad As a Wet Hen and Other Funny Idioms*. New York, N.Y.: Clarion Books, 1987.

White, E.B. *Charlotte's Web*. New York, N.Y.: Harper, 1952.

Zemach, M. *The Three Little Pigs*. New York, N.Y.: Farrar, Straus & Giroux, 1988.

Zion, G. *Harry, the Dirty Dog*. New York, N.Y.: Harper, 1976.

Children's Literature about Disabilities

Adams, B. *Like It Is: Facts and Feelings about Handicaps from Kids Who Know*. New York, N.Y.: Walker, 1979.

Aiello, B. & J. Shulman, J. *Business Is Looking Up*. Frederick, Md.: Twenty-First Century Books, 1988.

Aiello, B. & J. Shulman. *It's Your Turn at Bat*. Frederick, Maryland: Twenty-First Century Books, 1988.

Bergman T. *We Laugh, We Love, We Cry: Children Living with Mental Retardation*. Milwaukee, Wisc.: Gareth Stevens Press, 1989.

Bergman, T. *Going Places: Children Living with Cerebral Palsy*. Milwaukee, Wisc.: Gareth Stevens Press, 1991.

Booth, B.D. & J. Lamarche. *Mandy*. New York, N.Y.: Lothrop, Lee & Shepard, 1991.

Callen, L. *Sorrow's Song*. Boston, Mass.: Little Brown, 1979.

Clifton, L. *My Friend Jacob*. New York, N.Y.: E.P. Dutton, 1980.

Corrigan, K. *Emily Umily*. Toronto, Ont.: Annick Press, 1984.

Damrell, L. *With the Wind*. New York, N.Y.: Orchard Books, 1991.

Gaitskell, S. *A Story of Jean*. Toronto, Ont.: Oxford University Press, 1989.

Goldin, B. D. *Cakes and Miracles*. New York, N.Y.: Penguin, 1991.

Gutman, B. *Jim Abbott, Star Pitcher*. Brookfield, Conn.: The Millbrook Press, 1992.

Lasker, J. *Nick Joins In*. New York, N.Y.: Albert Whitman, 1980.

Laura, D. *We Can Do It*. Chicago, Ill.: Checkerboard Press, 1990.

Litchfield, A.B. *A Cane in Her Hand*. Chicago, Ill.: Albert Whitman, 1977.

Marek, M. *Different Not Dumb*. New York, N.Y.: Franklin Watts, 1985.

Radin, R.Y. *Carver*. New York, N.Y: Macmillan, 1990.

Raskin, E. *The Spectacles*. New York, N.Y.: Atheneum, 1988.

Rosenberg, M.B. *My Friend Leslie*. New York, N.Y.: Lothrop, Lee & Shepard, 1983.

Roy, R. *Move Over, Wheelchairs Coming Through: Seven Young People in Wheelchairs Talk about Their Lives*. New York, N.Y.: Houghton Mifflin, 1985.

Shyer, M.F. Welcome Home, Jellybean. New York, N.Y.: Charles Scribner's, 1982.

Slepian, J. *The Alfred Summer*. New York, N.Y.: Macmillan, 1980.

. . . .

RESOURCES

Additional Professional Reading

Anderson, C.C. & M.F. Apseloff. *Nonsense Literature for Children: Aesop to Seuss*. Hamden, Conn.: Shoestring Press, 1989.

Barrs, M. & A. Thomas (eds.). The Reading Book. Markham, Ont.: Pembroke, 1993.

Gold, J. *Read for Your Life: Literature As a Life Support System*. Markham, Ont.: Fitzhenry and Whiteside, 1990.

Golick, M. *Playing with Words*. Markham, Ont.: Pembroke, 1987.

Graves, M. *A Word Is a Word...or Is It?* New York, N.Y.: Scholastic, 1985.

Kropp, P. *The Reading Solution: Making Your Child a Reader for Life*. New York, N.Y.: Random House, 1993.

McGee, L.M. & D.J. Richgels. *Literacy's Beginnings: Supporting Young Readers and Writers*. Boston, Mass.: Allyn & Bacon, 1990.

Razinski, T.V. & C.S. Gillespie. *Sensitivity Issues: An Annotated Guide to Children's Literature K-6*. Phoenix, Ariz.: Ornyx Press, 1992.

Rex, E.J., A.J. Koenig, D.P. Wormsley & R.L. Baker. *Foundations of Braille Literacy*. New York, N.Y.: American Foundation for the Blind Press, 1994.

Roeher Institute. *Teachers Helping Teachers: Problem-Solving Teams That Work*. Video and manual illustrating problem-solving using teams of teachers. North York, Ont.: The Roeher Institute, 1994.

Computer Resources

SOFTWARE

Letter Names, Sounds and Spelling

Alphabet Blocks: Bright Star Technology

Letters and Words

Connection: IBM's Writing to Read: A highly structured spelling program for five- to eight-year-olds. Illustrates phonetic spelling with animation and pictures.

Goofy's Word Factory: Walt Disney Computer Software

The Mickey Mouse Series: Walt Disney Computer Software. For three- to seven-year-olds. No wrong answers. Press a key and an object associated with Mickey Mouse appears on-screen.

Reader Rabbit: The Learning Company. For three- to eight-year-olds. Macintosh version includes color graphics and sound.

Spellbound: The Learning Company. For seven- to 12-year-olds. Includes four entertaining games with predefined spelling lists. Customized lists can be created.

Word Processing and Writing

Bank Street Writer Plus: Broderbund Software or Scholastic Software. A beginning word-processing program for seven- to 10-year-olds. Offers large print.

Davidson's Kid Works: Davidson and Associates. A writing program for children from four to 10. Illustrations included. Can be used to create rebus games, puzzles and stories.

Writer Rabbit: The Learning Company. A mix of games and animation. Provides opportunities to practice sentence construction.

Talking Once upon a Time: Compu-Teach Educational Software. For six- to 10-year-olds. Includes illustrations. Uses keys to move bits of artwork on the screen.

Software with Synthetic Speech Features

The Talking Screen: Words+. Operated with a switch. Features graphic and high-quality synthetic speech and print to begin the process of auditory scanning. An area of the monitor is illuminated as selections are heard. New items can be added and the screen can be programmed for specific activities. Words, sentences, rhymes, songs, the alphabet and numerals are included. A flexible program that can be adjusted to meet the needs of individual students.

The Talking Stickybear Alphabet: Weekly Reader Software. Teaches names and sounds of letters.

The Talking Alpha Chimp: Orange Cherry Software. Teaches the names and sounds of letters.

Talking Tiles: Bright Star Technology. Combines sounds with letter symbols.

Dr. Peete's Talk/Writer: Hartley Courseware. Combines sounds with letter symbols.

Reading Riddles: Pelican Software. A vocabulary program for beginning readers.

Construct A Word I and II: Developmental Learning Materials. For seven to 11-year-olds. Students both see and hear how vowels and consonants, digraphs and diphthongs combine to make words.

Syllasearch I, II, III: Developmental Learning Materials. Provide experience with word analysis by progressing from simple high-frequency words to words of four syllables.

Once upon a Time: Compu-Teach. Teaches story-writing and illustrating.

Pow! Zap! Ker-Plunk! The Comic Book Maker: Pelican Software. Teaches story-writing and illustrating.

Toystore: Don Johnston Development. Includes interactive stories.

BRAILLE DISPLAYS

Braille Lite and *Braille 'n Speak*: Blazie Engineeering. Electronic devices that connect to a computer by way of serial or parallel cables. Often combined with other hardware and software to make up an integrated unit.

In addition, special computer screens have been designed for children with visual impairments. These reduce the number of items shown and increase the width, boldness of lines and the space around displayed items.

Alternative input systems include a variety of adjustments that permit the computer to read Morse code and make use of speech synthesizers and switches.

Switches provide an alternative to the standard keyboard and are operated using the hand or head. The placement and sensitivity of the switch is adjustable so that very little movement is required. Single or dual switches are available.

Unicorn Keyboard: Unicorn Engineering. A programmable keyboard with 128 touch-sensitive areas. Custom keyboard layouts can be stored on disk and new overlays can be created. The size of the keys can be tailored to the specific needs of individuals.

Touch Window: Sunburst Communications. A pressure-sensitive transparent plastic screen that fits over the monitor. May be used as a touch screen, graphics tablet, input pad or interactive book pad. Both the Unicorn Keyboard and Touch Window can be used with speech synthesizers.

MORE TITLES FROM THE PIPPIN TEACHER'S LIBRARY

Helping Teachers Put Theory into Practice

STORYWORLDS: LINKING MINDS AND IMAGINATIONS
THROUGH LITERATURE
Marlene Asselin, Nadine Pelland, John Shapiro

Using literature to create rich opportunities for learning.

WHOLE LANGUAGE: PRACTICAL IDEAS
Mayling Chow, Lee Dobson, Marietta Hurst, Joy Nucich

*Down-to-earth suggestions for both shared and independent reading
and writing, with special emphasis on evaluation strategies.*

THE WHOLE LANGUAGE JOURNEY
Sara E. Lipa, Rebecca Harlin, Rosemary Lonberger

*Making the transition to a literature-based, child-centered
approach to learning.*

WRITING PORTFOLIOS:
A BRIDGE FROM TEACHING TO ASSESSMENT
Sandra Murphy, Mary Ann Smith

*How portfolios can help students become active partners
in the writing process.*

THE FIRST STEP ON THE LONGER PATH:
BECOMING AN ESL TEACHER
Mary Ashworth

*Practical ideas for helping children who are learning
English as a second language.*

SUPPORTING STRUGGLING READERS
Barbara J. Walker

*Building on struggling readers' strengths to help them broaden
their strategies for making sense of text.*

ORAL LANGUAGE FOR TODAY'S CLASSROOM
Claire Staab

*Integrating speaking and listening into the curriculum to help
children discover the power of language.*

AN EXCHANGE OF GIFTS:
A STORYTELLER'S HANDBOOK
Marion V. Ralston

*Imaginative activities to enhance language programs
by promoting classroom storytelling.*

THE WORD WALL: TEACHING VOCABULARY
THROUGH IMMERSION
Joseph Green

*Using mural dictionaries—word lists on walls—to strengthen
children's reading, speaking and writing skills.*

INFOTEXT: READING AND LEARNING
Karen M. Feathers

*Classroom-tested techniques for helping students overcome
the reading problems presented by informational texts.*

WRITING IN THE MIDDLE YEARS
Marion Crowhurst

*Suggestions for organizing a writing workshop approach
in the classroom.*

AND THEN THERE WERE TWO:
CHILDREN AND SECOND LANGUAGE LEARNING
Terry Piper

*Insights into the language-learning process help
teachers understand how ESL children become bilingual.*

IN ROLE: TEACHING AND LEARNING DRAMATICALLY
Patrick Verriour

*A leading drama educator demonstrates how easily drama can be used
to integrate learning across the curriculum.*

LINKING MATHEMATICS AND LANGUAGE: PRACTICAL
CLASSROOM ACTIVITIES
Richard McCallum, Robert Whitlow

*Practical, holistic ideas for linking language—both reading
and writing—and mathematics.*

TEACHING THE WORLD'S CHILDREN
Mary Ashworth, H. Patricia Wakefield

*How early childhood educators and primary teachers can help
non-English-speaking youngsters use—and learn—English.*

THE MONDAY MORNING GUIDE TO COMPREHENSION
Lee Gunderson

*Strategies for encouraging students to interact with,
rather than react to, the information they read.*

LOOK AT ME WHEN I TALK TO YOU:
ESL LEARNERS IN NON-ESL CLASSROOMS
Sylvia Helmer, Catherine Eddy

*How culture influences the messages we give—and receive—
and how this affects classroom practice.*

PARTNERSHIPS IN LEARNING:
TEACHING ESL TO ADULTS
Julia Robinson, Mary Selman

*Practical ideas for forming rewarding partnerships with adult
ESL learners.*

SO...YOU WANT TO TEACH ADULTS?
Elizabeth Williams

*An adult educator explores collaborative philosophies and techniques
that work with adult learners.*

AN ENGLISH TEACHER'S SURVIVAL GUIDE:
REACHING AND TEACHING ADOLESCENTS
Judy S. Richardson

*The story of an education professor who returns to a high-school
classroom determined to put theory into practice.*